# The Dirty Boots

## THE STORIES OF A RELUCTANT WARRIOR

*To Bud,*
*John F. Holm*
*From an ex Navy corpsman.*
*Travel safely shipmate.*
*"Doc"*

## John F. Holm

D0873532

Order this book online at www.trafford.com
or email orders@trafford.com

Most Trafford titles are also available at major online book retailers.

Printed in the United States of America.

ISBN: 978-1-4669-4825-9 (sc)
ISBN: 978-1-4669-4827-3 (hc)
ISBN: 978-1-4669-4826-6 (e)

Library of Congress Control Number: 2012913425

*Trafford rev. 07/25/2012*

 www.trafford.com

North America & international
toll-free: 1 888 232 4444 (USA & Canada)
phone: 250 383 6864 ♦ fax: 812 355 4082

# ACKNOWLEDGMENTS

A few special people come to mind when I think of whom to thank for making this project a reality.

My sons, Peter John and Andrew Christian, for encouraging me to write down my memories. Both have also been helpful when I fought with the computer.

Neitcha Valor for being at the right place at the right time to give a lot of computer help.

My sister-in-law, Dr. Stephanie Myers Schim, who took a part of her vacation time to do a read—through. She offered several good suggestions for clarity and helped fix some loose ends.

A wonderful friend and neighbor, Teresa Misco, MALS, for her editorial assistance, creative energy, encouragement, and moral support. She never changed a story and helped me make them easier to read.

The men who served with me, who inspired these stories and kept me alive to tell them. They will always be my heroes.

My loving wife and special friend, Harriet, who endured the process of this project in both time and clutter, who knew me before and loved me after, and has shared my life for forty-eight years.

Dedication

To my fallen comrades.

# CONTENTS

## I

## II

# I

## LIFE BEFORE VIETNAM

I have often said that there is a very thin line between heroism and stupidity; sometimes, only the final outcome determines the name by which it may be called if you survive it or if you don't. Recently, I have read others' recollections of some of the same situations that I will describe. It has shown me that people see a given situation slightly differently depending on who they are, where they are standing, and what they are doing at the time. I am sure that their accounts are just as accurate from their vantage point as I have tried to make mine. Since these stories are about me and it is a family history, you should probably know what led up to the events that follow.

After keeping my mother awake all night, I was finally born around eight in the morning of June 22, 1947, in Three Rivers, Michigan. It was here that I lived with my parents and two younger brothers, James D. and Jack A. Holm, a black and white English Setter named Lady, assorted cats, goldfish, turtles, and birds. Our paternal grandparents lived not too far away in our town. Our maternal grandparents lived on a farm a few miles outside town. We visited often with them, as well as with many aunts, uncles, and cousins. My father was a master machinist and worked in a factory, and when we boys were older, Mom worked in a "five-and-ten-cent store." We were the kind of hardworking, blue-collar, middle-class American family that was very typical in our country during the post-World War II, "Cold War" years—a politically turbulent time during which the communist countries, led by the Soviet Union and China, and the noncommunist countries, led by the United States and most European nations, were trying to exert their power and ideals upon smaller countries around the world. Each side kept making rockets and atomic bombs, trying to be bigger and stronger, in hopes that the developing countries would choose to be like them. It truly was the biggest-kids-on-the-block-fighting-with-each-other scenario. Instead of actually fighting themselves, they used the smaller kids as pawns. They should have been working together to make the neighborhood a nice, safe place for everybody.

We lived in a two-story white house on a street lined with maple trees, across from our grade school, and only five blocks from the high school. We walked to school every day. Although it was not really uphill both ways, in the heavy Michigan snows, there were times it seemed that way. I was a cub scout and a school crossing guard on the corner of our street. I attended the Ninth Street Methodist church regularly and had a newspaper route for six years. I won the Inland Daily Press Newspaper Boy of the Year award twice during that time. I also played the coronet in the high school band, for which I earned my high school letters. I was notably not athletic, so receiving a letter in sports was not likely to happen. I was a fat, uncoordinated bookworm, who, during my sophomore year, stood five feet five inches tall and weighed 225 pounds. I had a few good friends but was never really a part of the "in crowd." I studied hard, had a solid B grade point average, and because of a small part in the senior play, earned just enough extracurricular points to graduate from high school with honors.

In November of my junior year of high school, President John F. Kennedy was shot and killed in Dallas, Texas. The new President, Lyndon Johnson, began increasing our troop strength in what was being called a "police action" in Vietnam. It was really a civil war between the communist-backed north and democracy-supported south. It was happening at a time when young people in their teens and early twenties had been challenged by President Kennedy to make a difference. In his inaugural address, he said, "Ask not what your country can do for you. Ask what you can do for your country."

This became the country's youth mantra.

Many in my generation became very interested in the political process and formed opinions that did not always agree with the current policies. The civil rights movement was gaining momentum, women were becoming more liberated, and humans were preparing for the first steps on the moon. The nightly news was filled with images of large groups of young people demonstrating in the streets. Sometimes this was peaceful and sometimes not. From the battlefields of Vietnam came daily film footage of helicopters, explosions, and dead and dying soldiers. Truly, this was a time of change and growth in our country, complete with the inevitable growing pains.

Because I did not really want to be in a war and the military draft could be deferred for higher education, I applied to college and was accepted at both Western Michigan University and Central Michigan University. I chose the latter but did not do very well there. I was a small-town boy in a big school, with poor study habits and no specific goals. I did, however, meet a wonderful young woman, a dark-haired, hazel-eyed beauty with fantastic legs. When picking her up at her dorm, I would sit where the first part of her I always saw were her beautiful legs coming down the stairway. Her name was Harriet, and she would one day become my wife, but that was still a few years away.

## JOIN THE NAVY AND SEE THE WORLD

After two semesters, my poor grades made the possibility of being drafted a very real concern again. During World War II, my father had been on a Navy Destroyer in the Pacific. Since I had seen no blue or white uniforms on the six o'clock news in recent jungle combat footage, I went to the Navy Reserve Station in Kalamazoo and enlisted. I also enrolled at Southwestern Michigan Community College.

I did much better in a smaller school setting but still had no specific career goal in mind. So I got to thinking, which historically had seldom worked out the way I had planned it. My Navy pretest scores were high, and I could choose from many assignments. I had some interest in the field, so I decided to try medicine. That way I could experience the work, find out if it was something I really wanted to do, earn some money and GI education benefits that would allow me to continue with college, and stay out of Vietnam. If I did go, at least I would be offshore on a ship with three hot meals a day and a clean, dry bed.

## HOSPITAL CORPS SCHOOL

During the spring semester in college, I applied for and was accepted into Hospital Corps School, Class 86-67 in San Diego, California. This allowed me to finish the semester and begin my two years of active duty. Corps School was sixteen weeks of intensive training, shortened to fourteen weeks by adding night classes; more Corpsmen were needed because of the troop buildup in Vietnam. I learned many interesting things, like the fact that our enlisted men's club, The Pink Palace (only in California), so named because of the pink color of the stucco covering it, was the place where Bill Cosby, one of my favorite comedians, had performed when he went to Navy Corps School. Liberty was usually spent teaching myself to play the guitar and going to the San Diego Zoo or Balboa Park. Both were just across the street from the hospital/school complex.

Our company nurse instructor was Lt. Commander M. A. Coefield. We all referred to her as "Ma Coefield," with a great deal of respect, but not to her face. She was a very good instructor who had congenital amblyopia (also known as lazy eye), which in her case was not a good name for her condition. While her eyes did not track together, she could see equally well from either one. We got away with nothing in her classroom.

The person with the highest overall grade point average was the "Honor Man" of the company. He could pick his next duty assignment after school. Great Lakes Naval Hospital in Chicago was very close to home so I really wanted to be Honor Man. I studied very hard and came very close. I was the third highest out of forty and only missed the mark by 0.12 points. This was not too bad considering we had three college graduates, and the average educational level in my company was over two years of college.

About half way through school, I heard someone say, "After graduation, the whole company is going to FMF training."

"What's that mean?" I asked, not trusting any military anachronism containing MF.

"Fleet Marine Force School, man."

"Again. What's that mean?"

"That's where they teach us to be mini-marines."

"Why would I want to do something like that?"

"Don't you know anything, man? Navy corpsmen also serve as combat medics in the Marines."

"No, I didn't know that. So how do I change jobs?"

"You don't want to do that, man. Rumor has it that hospital corps school dropouts or washouts (failures) are sent straight to swift boat duty in Vietnam."

## FLEET MARINE FORCE MEDIC

That certainly did not sound like something I wanted to do, so in September and October of 1967 it was off to Oceanside at Camp Pendleton, where we were issued our first set of green fatigues and met our next set of instructors.

Drill Sergeant Green and his staff were a mix of Marines and corpsmen, all with recent experience in Vietnam. Sergeant Green, an African American, could easily have been featured on a recruiting poster. Over six feet tall, just standing still in his crisp utility uniform, he inspired confidence.

The training was very demanding, both physically and mentally, because they knew what they were training us for. The higher our level of preparedness, the better were the chances of our survival and of the troops in our care. We marched or ran in formation to meals, classes, everywhere. We learned basic battlefield tactics and the language of combat so we could act and react as part of a fighting unit. We studied the basics of nuclear, biological, and chemical warfare, along with map reading, and building field latrines and showers. Compass navigation, evasion techniques, and how to eat off the land were also part of the training.

Then came the medical part, learning how to give the most and best treatment to the men in our units with the resources we could carry or what was naturally available. We learned how to make a splint out of wood from an ammo box, a tree limb, a rifle, or even how to use an unbroken leg to immobilize a fractured one. Cellophane from a cigarette pack or C-rations could make an airtight patch over a sucking chest wound. We learned these and many other bits of knowledge, some of which I have continued to find useful over the years.

We spent hours practicing treatment drills, where half of us were the corpsmen and the other half played the wounded. As a casualty, you were assigned a wound or injury and would be lying on the ground alongside the "grinder" (an asphalt-covered area behind the barracks where we also practiced marching). As a corpsman you ran up to your patient, read the slip of paper that listed the wound/injury (it was assumed that some injuries would be so severe the man could not speak) and treat the injury. We did all this while the instructors walked up and down the line watching our work and constantly advising:

"Keep your head and body down."

"The wounded man may be your only cover."

"Keep him between yourself and the incoming fire."

"He is already shot and you're not."

"You are of no use to your men if you're dead."

We ran this drill over and over and over, both in daylight and darkness. When we became good at it, we were taken out into the field to do it some more. Of course to get to the practice field/camping area, we packed our tents and equipment on our backs and marched in. The terrain was similar to the set where they filmed M*A*S*H* with dry hills and lots of sagebrush. We set up a camp, ate C-rations, and went through the drills again and again. Now each time we practiced, we had the added effect of being harassed by an aggressor force. Playing the roll of the enemy soldiers were men that had returned from Vietnam.

Corps School in San Diego had taught us how to take care of people in a nice, clean situation. Field Medical Service School at Camp Pendleton taught us how to do the job under much more adverse conditions. We were often in awkward and uncomfortable positions, using only what could be carried or made, all while being tired and a bit frightened. They made it as real as possible, and every one of us hoped that we would never have to use this knowledge.

We had been issued M14 rifles adapted to fire blank rounds, and if we were attacked, we could fire back. We were not really expected to take any offensive action, but nobody said we could not. One evening we came under attack from a very small number of individuals. *What the heck*, I thought. Combat does not have any hard and fast rules. My position was far to their left, so I would try to outflank them. Using the stealth skills taught to me by my father and grandfather while hunting, I was able to come up behind them, unseen. I "shot" one and captured the other two. Of course the advisors made me give them back, but it did feel good to score one for our side. We experienced the normal scratches and bruises from physical activity in rough terrain. The only real casualties on this drill occurred when a few of the men got lice from their sleeping bags. Fortunately, I was not one of them.

It was not all work, and we did get some time off. We were near the town of Oceanside, California, which had a train station. One weekend liberty I went into town and caught the Amtrak train to Anaheim where I made my first visit to Disneyland. For a kid from the Midwest, this was a dream come true. I did several of the rides. *Pirates of the Caribbean* and *It's a Small World* were new back then. I also toured a few of the stationary venues and really liked the 360-degree theater. Suffice it to say, I had a wonderful time, even though I had to leave early to catch the train back and missed the famous Disney evening parade and fireworks.

A couple of weeks later Disney had an Armed Forces Day. They closed the park to all but military personnel and their families, so I was able to go a second time. This time I traveled in a semi-truck trailer, which had been modified to carry troops. There were bench seats added along both sides and down the center, with open holes cut out near the roof serving as air conditioners. We called them cattle cars.

The park was just as much fun as the first time, although there was one small disappointment. Louis Armstrong, the great trumpet player, had been scheduled to perform on the Bourbon

Street stage, but he had become ill. For the record, I did make it back to Disneyland a third time with my wife and two sons several years later. This time we were able to stay for the parade of lights and fireworks show. From my experience, it is indeed a magical kingdom at any age.

Graduation from FMF training was soon coming, and we filled out our "dream sheets" requests for next duty station. *So I got to thinking* it would make more sense for them to assign east coast personnel to assignments in the Atlantic or Europe. *A lot less expensive to take someone already on the west coast for assignment to Vietnam*, I reasoned. I picked three east coast duty stations and received orders to the Naval Hospital, Camp Le Jeune, in North Carolina.

After six months of arduous training, Company 86-67 was breaking up. We said good-bye to new friends and boarded buses to various train stations, bus terminals, and airports as we spread out across the country. The only other sailor in the company from Michigan was Ken Hollis, and because bed assignments were made alphabetically, we shared a bunk. He was African American and lived in Detroit. His neighborhood was not quite in the projects, but he could see them from his front porch. I promised I would try and get together with him while on leave. He was taking the Amtrak home, and I was going to fly.

I boarded the bus that was going to the Los Angeles airport. Soon after purchasing my standby ticket, I was on my way home. The weather in southern California was sunny and hot, and we were in dress white uniforms. The weather reports for southern Michigan was heavy snow, so somewhere over the mountains of Colorado I went into the bathroom and changed into the dress blues I had in my carry-on bag. The stewardess in my section was a bit confused when she came back with my meal.

"Weren't you in a white uniform a few minutes ago?"

"Yes. I understand it is a bit colder in Chicago than it was in Los Angeles."

After a short layover in Chicago, followed by a short flight over Lake Michigan, I arrived in Kalamazoo, where the temperature was in the low twenties and the snow was blowing sideways. I walked down the stairs and across the tarmac to the terminal. My family was there to greet me. It was good to be home.

For the next thirty days I rested, ate Mom's home cooking, and visited with family and friends. I also drove to Detroit and visited with Harriet and her family, as well as my buddy Ken. Harriet drove us to his home, as she knew her way around better than I did. Detroit was recovering from the six-day race riots a few months before. It had been a very bad time for the people of this proud city, and there was still some tension in the air. We had a nice visit with Ken and his parents, but even they said it would be safer if we were on our way before nightfall. My thirty days of leave went by all too quickly. Soon I was repacking my bags and heading for my new job.

## CAMP LE JEUNE NAVAL HOSPITAL

Le Jeune was a good duty station. My assignment was pediatrics—working with the children of servicemen and women. It was like a regular job. We rotated shifts a week at a time, with day shift taking weekend liberty, while the evening and night crews worked twelve-hour shifts over the weekend. In this way, I was off every third weekend. When money permitted, I was able to make a trip back to Michigan. We called it "swooping" home for the weekend. On Friday afternoons, all the swoopers would go to the base library parking lot, where, for the cost of helping with gas, we could catch a ride in any direction. It was seldom that a ride was going as far as Michigan, but Ohio or Pennsylvania was often possible. I would have my ride drop me off at a truck stop on or near Interstate 80, and it was easy to find a trucker headed west who wanted someone to talk to and help him stay awake through the night. For most of them, company policy prohibited picking up hitchhikers, but many were willing to bend that rule for a serviceman. By sunrise I was usually in Detroit, catching a ride from the industrial area in the southern part of the city. Getting to the suburb of Berkley, where Harriet lived, was often the hardest part of the trip. I would have the better part of Saturday through Sunday with Harriet and would catch a late night flight back to base.

I lived in a twelve-man barracks, a large room divided into six two-man cubicles with the creative placement of beds and lockers. Bill, a burly redhead, was one of my barracks mates, and I would meet him again later as one of the First Platoon's corpsman in Charlie Company. Dave, a dark-haired, likable Pennsylvanian, and I occupied one of the two middle cubicles. John, a short fellow from Wisconsin, and Ron, a tall blond guy with a black belt in karate, had the other center space. The four of us became good friends, even though we all worked on different wards in the hospital and had different schedules. When our schedules permitted, we could usually be found hanging out doing something together.

The boathouse was just up the road on what was known as hospital point. Sometimes we would rent a couple of canoes and chase the alligators that lived in the New River and swamp. On one occasion, I came upon a ten-foot-long cottonmouth sunning itself across the path. Since we needed to go down this trail, I did the only thing I thought prudent at the time. I killed it with my K-Bar jungle knife. We took the snake, minus his head, back to the barracks, where I skinned it. As a practical joke, we made up some blood slides, added a fictional patient name, and sent them off to the lab. The lab folks were darn good; they diagnosed it right off as frog blood (close enough). It seems that all reptiles have a nucleus in their red blood cells. I stretched out the skin and pinned it to a board to dry, intending to make it into a guitar strap. While I thought I had found a safe place for it to cure, I was wrong. Someone swiped it.

On some days we would rent outboard motorboats and go down to the Atlantic. There was a small rural gas station and bait shop at one point, where a bridge crossed the river. We picked up food and beverages for lunch on the beach. On some days the Marines provided us with entertainment by practicing amphibious landings; on other days we would just go clamming.

One day I swam out to a rather large sandbar in the river. After exploring it for clams, I noticed it was becoming significantly smaller. I was a good distance from shore and a fairly stiff breeze was blowing, so while my friends could see me, they were unable to hear what I was saying. I yelled repeatedly for them to bring the boat out. So I got to thinking I'm a reasonably good swimmer, and I had gotten myself out here, so I began swimming back to shore. I underestimated the strength of the tide and current. I was used to inland lakes and rivers. About three-quarters of the way back, I realized I was in big trouble. By this time, I was only about a hundred yards from shore, and my buddies could finally hear me. They launched the boat and kept me from drowning.

Dave, who would frequently surprise us, returned from one of his "swoops" married. Another time he came back with a car, which gave us access to another form of cheap entertainment, the drive-in movies. There was a great little Deli/Sub shop just off base, where we would stop and get made-to-order sandwiches. Then we would stop at the supermarket and pick up chips and a six-pack and take in the movie on a dollar-a-car night.

One off day when I was sleeping, the Duty Officer called the barracks. One of the doctors on my ward had requested that I accompany a seriously ill infant to the Bethesda Naval Hospital for neurosurgery. I was honored that he had picked me even though my sleep was disturbed. I was a bit worried about the responsibility and really hoped that nothing would go wrong.

I experienced my very first helicopter ride on a UH 46 Sea Knight with a critically ill baby girl only days old. On the two-hour flight over Virginia, she needed her vital signs monitored, two diaper changes, and a bottle. The crew was intrigued and watched my every move. The trip went off well, and I transferred her safely to the corpsmen at Bethesda.

The trip home was more relaxed. I even took some pictures from the air. I ended up taking two more of these trips while stationed there, one to Walter Reed Army Hospital and the other to Newport Naval Hospital. The last trip I made from there involved a newborn with Tetralogy of Fallot, a rare birth problem that includes three separate heart defects. He was taken to University Hospital at Duke, but this time in a regular ambulance with a doctor and me. This child made the trip and survived the surgery, as did the others, so all the trips had happy endings.

Another interesting event occurred on one off-duty day when a local news station wanted to recreate a helicopter medical evacuation, dust-off, Vietnam style. I was volunteered again, and as it turned out, I played the part of a wounded Marine with my head wrapped in bandages. I coached the Marines from my stretcher on how the corpsman would handle the situation. That evening I watched myself on the six o'clock news—my two minutes of fame and glory with most of my face concealed in gauze bandages stained with Betadine.

In another brush with fame, my gloved hands are in a medical journal or textbook somewhere, holding a little guy who was born without all of his skin. Then it was called agenesis of the dermis (now termed Focal Dermal Hypoplasia Syndrome or Goltz Syndrome), which is another very rare birth defect. He had the necessary body and head skin, but on both arms and legs, he was only partially covered. We treated the condition as if it was a severe burn case, in sterile isolation, to prevent infection and moist dressings to keep the muscle tissue from drying out. We placed tiny strips of sterilized parachute silk between his fingers and toes so that as his dermis (skin) grew in, it would not web them together. Eventually, all his skin grew in by itself, and he went home with his complete hide.

Camp Le Jeune was a very large base with many residents and a lot of babies being born to the servicemen and their wives. While all of the normal healthy infants were cared for in the nursery, the children born with problems came to the pediatric unit where I worked. During my stay there, I saw some rather amazing and unusual birth problems. We had two patients that were born with intestinal tracts that were too short, and they had no way of having a bowel movement. Even in these tiny patients, our Navy surgeons were able to locate a circular muscle between the buttocks where the intestine should exit. Then going up into the abdomen, they would then actually pull the "dead-ended" intestine through this muscle. In time these kids would have normally functioning bodies. I know that my experiences on that floor had a lot to do with my later decision to go into the nursing profession.

It was now April, and so I got to thinking again that time was definitely in my favor; as of May I had a year of active duty time, and with the thirty days leave I had on the books, there was no way I could pull a full tour of duty in Vietnam. I might even just stay here at Le Jeune to finish out my time.

The middle of May rolled around, and with it the orders started to come in for our gang. Bill had just left for Vietnam; Ron was going to the US Naval Hospital, Bethesda, Maryland; John was assigned to the US Naval Hospital, Bremerton, Washington; Dave was headed to the USS Vulcan (an ammo ship in the Atlantic Fleet.) Then mine arrived. I was on my way to the 3rd Marine Division, reinforced, Republic of Vietnam. My reverse psychology ploy of volunteering every month had not worked. I had thought that anybody so crazy as to volunteer was probably going to act like John Wayne, get killed, and not be any good to anyone and so would not be sent to Vietnam. Besides, I was too short (in time left) to serve a full tour when I stopped. They had figured out my scam.

I spent June on leave and celebrated my twenty-first birthday by taking Harriet out to dinner at one of our favorite restaurants, "The Fox and Hounds." She was lovely in her yellow dress and upswept hair. Ever the performer, at one point she got up and sang "Summer Time" with the band. She had a beautiful lounge-singer voice.

Two days later we went to Kensington Park for a picnic, and before it was over, I had proposed. She did not give me an answer that day, and I let her know that I would be asking her again in a year when I came home. A week later I returned to Detroit, and we were again going out to dinner. As I parked the car and turned off the motor, she took a deep breath.

"Yes. I will marry you," she said.

Even though I had not expected to hear this from her so soon, the ring was in the glove compartment. Marriage plans would be contingent on my safe return, of course. But now she knew how much I loved her.

The day before my flight out, July 1, we went downtown to the Detroit River near Cobo Hall and sat on the side of a hill and watched the fireworks display. It was a joint celebration of July 4 and Canada's Freedom Day. It was well known that some Americans had already gone over the border to Canada to avoid being sent to Vietnam. Looking back, that might have been the wise thing to do. But having not done the wise thing up to this point, why start now?

The next day I boarded a plane and flew to California, and on July 3, I left the United States for Okinawa. It was a fourteen-hour flight, with a refueling stop in Hawaii. We were taken off the plane during the refueling stop, so I went with several others to the airport bar and enjoyed a beer. We flew over the International Dateline right about midnight, and it became the fifth. We had skipped right over July 4.

I really do not remember how long I stayed in Okinawa, probably three or four days, enough time for my body's internal clock to at least begin resetting. I was now twelve hours out of sync. I also began to acclimate to the heat and humidity.

I talked to a few men who were going the other direction, back to The World. They had completed their tours of duty. Basically, they did nothing to relieve my fears. Here, in layover mode, we received jungle uniforms and replaced our heavy combat boots with lighter weight jungle boots and made sure that all our paperwork and vaccinations were in order. I asked about a set of dog tags. Somehow, along the way, this had been overlooked at all my previous duty stations, even though I had asked at each one. "That problem would be handled when I arrived in Vietnam," I was told.

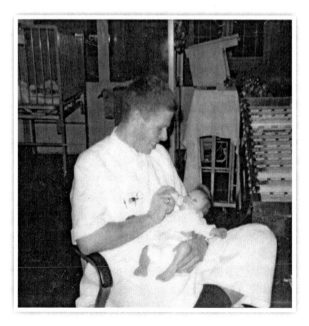

# II

## THE NAM

All too soon I found myself on another commercial airplane, flying over the South China Sea, on my way to Da Nang. My level of fear was climbing as we drew closer, and I was sure that as soon as the wheels hit the tarmac, somebody would be shooting at me. You can only imagine what was going through my mind when the 707 landed. As we hustled down the airline ladder, some crazy person with sergeant stripes stood at the bottom of the stairway.

"Fall into formation!" he barked.

"Make three lines and dress right!" He shouted the standard orders for alignment.

*Here we are*, I thought, *in a country at war, with the sun setting, my nerves on edge, and I am standing in a nice straight line, like a tin duck in a shooting gallery.* To make the analogy even more realistic, it was "Left face! Forward march!" We were all targets now marching in a nice straight row toward waiting buses. It was getting dark, and our short bus ride around the perimeter of the airport ended; we were nervous passengers unloading in an area of several standard military green army tents. Inside each tent were about twenty or so canvas cots. We were told to pick one and get some sleep, as our processing would begin in the morning. Sleep? Just who were they kidding? I had some major concerns. The only weapon I had was a K-Bar jungle knife, which probably was not going to be much good in a gunfight. I was in a country where, according to all the news reports, Americans like myself were being killed regularly. I had not seen anyone on guard duty anywhere, and I had looked. These only scratched the surface of my fears. At any moment, a Viet Cong wearing black pajamas could come running into the tent blasting away with an AK-47 and throwing satchel charges everywhere. I have not even mentioned the wild animals and snakes, but you can be sure they were on my mind. Before fatigue took over completely, I spent some time trying to assess my chances of surviving my first day "in country." Along with us FNGs, short for f—king new guys, there were others being transferred to different units, returning from rest and relaxation (R&R) leave, or, for some reason unknown to me, spending the night in this olive green motel. The main things that separated them from us were that they were sound asleep, and their boots, sitting under the cots, were scruffy and caked with red clay. For a moment, I wondered what those dirty boots had seen. As sleep finally took over, I made one major decision; I would watch and learn from the people who had lived long enough to have dirty boots.

As the sun came up, I awoke to the sounds of vehicle traffic and people walking about and "Goooooooooooood Morning, Vietnam" coming from every transistor radio around. Much to my surprise, I was still alive and in one piece. My worries were somewhat laughable in hindsight. I was on a very large base, located in a very large city, miles from any real shooting. Up the street was the bowling alley, the movie theater, a PX (Post Exchange) the size of Walmart Superstore but better stocked, and many other buildings of solid construction. This was an area call Freedom Hill. Things did not seem too different from any other military base I had ever been on back in the United States. Watching where the dirty boots walked, I soon found the bathroom and breakfast.

Back at the tents, we waited until someone with a clipboard finally came along giving directions.

"Everyone for the 3rd Marine Division, fall in over there."
He pointed toward a large hangar with open doors where several people were sitting on folding metal chairs at standard foldout-type tables. A man dressed in olive green called my name. He handed me a large manila envelope full of paperwork. "Go over and join those guys!" he gestured. It all occurred in the military's typical hurry-up-and-wait fashion. After some time had passed, we were told to board our aircraft. We all walked across the tarmac toward a plane, which was not the regular passenger 707 type I had been on up until now. This was a battleship gray, walk-up-the-tail-ramp-and-find-a-canvas-seat-along-the-wall kind of aircraft. It was a C-130, with no heat, no windows, and no in-flight movies. Supplies were stacked in the middle on wooden pallets. When we were all on board, the tail ramp closed and we began to taxi. I realized that I was now in the company of more young men with rifles and dirty boots than those who were unarmed and in clean clothing. I listened, watched, and learned.

Soon, the roar of the engines increased and we lifted off, heading north to an airport/city they were calling Dong Ha. I learned that Dong Ha was real Indian country (a place where the enemy was) and that planes landing there were often fired upon by mortars and/or small arms.

"When the plane lands, move off quickly and head for the terminal," someone said.

The worries and fears were again filling my mind, and the silence around me said more than words. I was not alone in my concerns. I was nervous but remembered that someone had said that when we landed, I should head for the terminal. Okay, the place did have a terminal, so things could not be too bad, *right?*

I don't know how long the flight took, but the pitch of the engines changed and the hydraulic sounds of the flaps and landing gear signaled our approach to the airport. We were still rolling as the tailgate of the plane lowered. I picked up my seabag and orders and ran along with a line of young men all headed for the "terminal."

Only a little bigger than a two-car garage, it was an earthen-floored, steel decking roofed, heavily sandbagged bunker. No check-in counter, no gift shop, no lights, no phone, and definitely no Hertz car rental. Looking back through the door, I could see that our plane had wasted no time in once again becoming airborne. I am certain they continued to roll while we got off and they pushed the supplies down the ramp. They were already lifting off the runway. Their mission had been accomplished in under two minutes of ground time without ever stopping.

Everyone stayed inside the shelter of the terminal until the plane/target was well on its way. Then in groups of two and three, we moved out of the relative protection of the terminal and walked briskly to the "gate," which was actually a hole in a three-strand barbed wire fence that looked like the wooden-posted fences around my grandparents' farm pastures. The number of us remaining in the bunker was getting very small. I asked a couple of soldiers with whom I had struck up a conversation earlier when I might expect someone to pick me up. I was to report in at Quang Tri. They kind of chuckled and directed me to come along with them to the road. I could see that we were at the edge of a base and town. There was a real gate with a guard shack to my right and serious perimeter wire, visible for a long way in both directions until it curved out of sight. They told me that they were stationed here at Dong Ha. Quang Tri was about twenty-five miles up the road to my left.

"So when does the transportation come along?" I asked.

"Stick out your thumb, man," one of them said.

Not even a full day in country, a seabag on my back, orders in hand, a K-Bar my only way to protect myself, and I was standing alongside Highway 1, also called the *Street of No Joy*. Yep! Scared out of my wits would be grossly understating my current state of mind. I really had no clue where I was or where I was headed. The guys in mud-covered boots had said to hold out a thumb, so I did. What they did not tell me was that if I had been able to find the helicopter landing zone inside the base, I probably could have hitched a flight instead of a jeep ride. Standing there alone, time passed very slowly. But it was not too long before a big olive green truck came out of the base, and I held out my thumb. It stopped.

"Where you headed, man?" the driver asked.

"Quang Tri," I stammered.

"Me too. Hop on board." I climbed in. I was a moving target, at least for now, and on my way to Quang Tri.

My confidence began to return, and I was even able to enjoy the ride up a long gray ribbon of crushed gravel. The sun was shining brightly. The radio was playing a familiar Beach Boys song on the AFVN (Armed Forces Vietnam) radio station, and we were rolling along at a decent speed leaving a wispy cloud of dust behind us.

Okay, the olive-colored convertible was an open "6 by," which was a large truck with two wheels on the front axle and four wheels on the rear axle. The radio station was not CKLW Detroit or WLS Chicago. The road could be mined, the person sitting beside me was not female, and there was a real possibility of being shot at or blown up. This was not quite cruising my favorite local strip on a sunny day with my sweetheart, but at least I was headed in the right direction, I hoped. This lush valley was a mile or so wide with a broad flat bottom that eventually extended to a three hundred by four hundred foot ridgeline on either side. There were few trees until the ridges; it was mostly brush and tall grasses in more colors of green than I had thought existed. Before too long, I could make out a tent city set low in the distance. Helicopters were moving in and out above it. A few more minutes, and we were at the gate; the driver asked directions to 3rd MAR DIVS area and took me there. Saying thanks, I grabbed my seabag as I hopped down from the truck. Can you believe I was still lugging that thing around? I waved and watched the driver pull away with his load of supplies.

Quang Tri was a M*A*S*H-like setting, only bigger and more updated. The hardbacked buildings were a skeleton of lumber, plywood floors, and internal walls, with the tent material stretched over all of it. Steel sheeting was added to the roofs, with sandbags tied to them to keep the winds from blowing them off. This downtown area was about four to six blocks large; each block had two rows of tents, five in each row, with a walkway in between and a road around each block. It was the area for war management: supply, payroll, communications, storage, transportation (which I thought was sorely lacking), armory, mail, mess hall, regimental aide station, record keeping of the living, wounded, and dead, etc. Many more of these hardback tents were used as barracks, classrooms, and lesser office spaces. They occupied another three or four blocks. The sounds of jeeps and trucks going about their daily business were mixed with the constant stationary motors of the generators, the *thwump thwump* of helicopters flying in and out, and the chatter of people going to and fro. The Marines, in an attempt to give this area a homier feel, had planted a few scraggly flowerbeds. No grass grew in the hard red clay, and the flowers were struggling to survive. Street signs, like Hollywood and Vine, had been posted on corners. Wooden sidewalks had been built from the boards of supply pallets or supply boxes. Rocks the size of softballs lined the edges of the streets like curbs.

I wondered about the four-by-four foot structures that resembled closets without houses. On the roof of each set, a fifty-five gallon steel barrel wrapped around a galvanized chimney. A homemade ladder was propped against the side of each closet. I later discovered that these were the showers. The chimney was attached to a submersible heater, while the ladder allowed one to carry buckets of water to the roof to fill the barrel. Once hot, the water was gravity fed with a basic on/off valve. Some had regular showerheads mailed from the United States. Others used recycled C-ration cans with nail holes punched in one end to create the shower. Do not ever underestimate the creativity of American troops bringing touches of home to their surroundings. I walked up the wooden sidewalks taking in this entirely strange new place. I found the headquarters building/tent and reported in.

The remainder of the day was spent trekking from one tent to another. I signed in at payroll, unloaded my seabag at the storage tent. I hit the equipment and medical tents and a few others, including personnel, where I again inquired about a set of dog tags. I left behind a trail of paperwork and signatures. I picked up a backpack, a rain poncho with a detachable liner (which was destined to become my tent/sleeping bag), a web belt with two canteens (I was assured that two would be enough), a flak jacket, helmet, extra socks, an olive green sweat shirt (which made no sense to me in the ninety plus degree heat), a nylon stretcher (just add tree limbs for the poles), my Unit One (a fanny pack about the size and shape of a half loaf of bread for small medical supplies and pills, emblazoned with a bright red cross), and an M1911 Colt 45 caliber pistol with ammunition. It was a busy day. On my second night in country, I was again sleeping in a transient tent awaiting my assignment. Even though I was much closer to danger, I felt strangely much more secure because I could see the perimeter and defenses and now, with a pistol, could actually defend myself.

"Goooooooooooooooooooooooooood Morning, Vietnam!"

The unofficial reveille of AFVN radio called out from multiple portable radios around me. I stumbled to the bathroom, made it to breakfast, and reported to the tent where I was to receive my unit assignment.

There were eight or ten of us corpsmen that morning. One of the guys was a San Diego Corps School classmate. We spent the next few minutes catching up on what had happened to each of us since school and waiting to be told what was coming next in our lives. We were called, one at a time, to the front of the tent. Since I was not the first, I sat down in the shade of the tent and waited with the others. As the first man came out the rear of the tent, he called out the name of the next to go in.

"What did you get?" was always the first question asked of the man coming out. Assignments were given in two numbers. The first indicated the battalion, and the second designated the regiment. Answers varied 1/5, 3/27, 2/ 7, and so on. The man would then receive "high fives," a pat on the back, and comments like "Way to go!" "All right!" and similar congratulatory statements.

By the time my turn came, I thought I had this routine all figured out. I walked in the front door, received my unit assignment, and signed the necessary paperwork. I was given the name of the next man to call in, and then I walked out the rear door.

"Tulley, you're next." I got 1/9. To my bewilderment, I was met with "Oh shit!" "Too bad!" "Sorry, man!"

Certainly, this was not what I had expected.

"All right. What's the matter with 1/9?"

Apparently working pediatrics. I had missed the stories the others had heard from the returning wounded that they had cared for. I was clueless. They quickly filled me in.

"Don't you know, man? The Ghost Battalion! The Walking Dead!"

"The NVA (North Vietnamese Army) has three or four regiments out looking for 1/9, and their primary objective is to wipe them out."

"1/9 gets overrun all the time. You can't even go to the crapper without getting overrun," they responded.

My education and fear now brought up to speed, I went back around to the front of the tent and up to the desk where I told the corporal that my good friend had just been assigned to 3/5 and that I would really like to go to that unit with him. Nothing ventured, nothing gained. It didn't work; I came out the back of the tent the second time with a feeling of impending doom.

The temperature and humidity were both in the high nineties. This whole country had an earthy smell of dead vegetation and dirty bathrooms, and a large number of the enemy forces were already looking for me with malice. I was not sure things could be much worse. I was told to catch a ride to join my unit in about thirty minutes' time. They were near a village named Cam Lo.

My thoughts racing at a mind-numbing pace, and with a lot of black polish still on my boots, I walked off to meet my fate.

"The Walking Dead" was a title and a warning from Hanoi Hanna, the "Tokyo Rose" of Vietnam, who broadcasted propaganda on the radio. She spoke English with very little accent, and her voice was soft and sultry. Between current popular songs from the United States, she would tell us how much our wives, girlfriends, and mothers missed us, and how our leaders were just using us to further their own ends. She often told us where we were located (she was only right about twenty-five percent of the time) and warned that "such and such" NVA Regiment was on its way to kill all of us.

"You are just dead men walking into our trap," she taunted.

She recommended that we refuse to fight for a cause that was not our own and listen to our friends back home who were protesting against the war. Our own intelligence gathering sources had intercepted information that at least three North Vietnamese commanders had promised to obliterate us as a birthday present to Ho Chi Minh. To the best of my knowledge, we were the only American unit with at least one NVA Regiment attached to our hip at all times.

# JOINING 1/9

Soon, I was sitting in a jeep, possibly heading for my very short future. This was another one of those times when the fears were running high. To be honest, I did not even know what to be worried about, so my mind jumped all over the place conjuring up all sorts of "boogeymen."

I do not recall if I knew how to find Charlie Company Second Platoon before I got there or if I was told after arriving. But find them I did. I reported in to Lieutenant Casey and Sergeant Ryder, and I met Doc Keith Sieb. A marine rifle platoon normally had two corpsmen assigned. Keith was a friendly guy with an unruly mop of sandy brown hair. He took me around and introduced me to the platoon. I met more faces and names than I could remember right then. Everyone was young, skinny, and dressed in green. In a very short time, however, I would know the name and/or nickname of each of them.

A full-strength platoon is about sixty men; we seemed to be around forty, and a quarter of these were replacements with shiny black boots. This supported the stories the others had told me back at Quang Tri. As I was meeting them, they let me know that they had a certain respect for corpsmen but that if I didn't do my job well, my replacement would. Since I knew the Navy was not planning on replacing me for a few months, it didn't take too much imagination to catch their meaning. They were going to do their job to the best of their ability, and they expected no less from me. Going to sleep on the bare ground with the second Platoon Command Post on my third night in country made the cots in the transient tents a pleasant memory—a luxury I would seldom experience during the rest of my time in Vietnam.

The following morning, I joined Doc Sieb for a breakfast of C-rations. We then made rounds on the whole platoon; this would be a daily routine for the next nine months. It was important for a few reasons. It provided an opportunity to check on the general health of each man and treat any minor maladies. It was also the job of the corpsman to hand out malaria prevention pills. Dapsone, a small white tablet, was taken once a day, every day. On Sunday, the "Big Orange Pill," a quinine derivative, accompanied it. At times when we were busy in the field, the "Big Orange Pill" also served as a reminder of which day of the week it was. After our rounds, we reported the overall health and mental status of the unit to Lieutenant Casey. I would then circulate among the troops getting to know them better. I soon became "Doc John."

The Battalion Surgeon and any other real physicians were officers and therefore called Sir or by their rank. All corpsmen were docs. My training did not come close to that of a physician, but having the men call me "Doc" was both humbling and burdensome. The title made me appreciate a responsibility to do everything in my power to protect them and not let them down. At this moment, however, I had no idea of how I might react in actual combat. Fight or flight?

I learned several phrases in the local language: *Didi:* to go fast or go away; *Didi mau*: you go away, when given as a direction; *Chu hoi*: to surrender, also used to describe someone who had surrendered i.e.: "He is a *Chu hoi* scout;" *Boo-coo*: many or much, probably from the French word beaucoup with the same meaning; *Dinky dau*: crazy. *Number One* meant something was very good. *Number Ten* meant something was very bad. *Toy bac-si:* I am a medic. This last one came in handy very early on because at some point in the day I walked by a six- or seven-year-old Vietnamese boy who was looking very intently at a scrape on his knee. I said, "*Toy bac-si.*" He let me wash off the scrape and apply some Bacitracin and a Band-Aid. Soon, I had two or three more children with nicks and scratches come over. I was feeling really good about myself at that point because I was being an ambassador of goodwill and really helping these kids. As I was on Band-Aid number eight or nine, I looked across the way and noticed my next patient intentionally cutting his finger on some barbed wire. I couldn't believe it; these children were so starved for attention that they would injure themselves for a Band-Aid and a kind word. Thus, I learned another of my lessons; war creates emotional casualties even in noncombatants. I closed up shop then and there and tried, by using a mock action of cutting myself and saying "Number 10, no!" to impress on them that they should not do this anymore. I'm not sure if it did any good.

A while later, we were given the order to "saddle up" (pick up your gear and put on your backpack, we are going somewhere). We climbed on the back of large trucks, like the one I rode in from Dong Ha to Quang Tri, and moved out. A few miles up the road they let us off, and we began "humping it" (the military term for moving on foot with all your gear on your back) into the countryside. Someone had said that earlier in the day a convoy had been shot at in this area. We were looking for the shooters. This was my first hump, and I do not know how far we walked. The temperature was again in the upper nineties, and so was the humidity. After about three hours, it had kicked my ass. I focused my eyes on the backpack of the Marine in front of me and called on every bit of energy I had to keep putting one foot in front of the other. I was on autopilot, and both of my canteens were empty. I had tried to be conservative, but by the time we stopped for the night, I was already moderately dehydrated. When we were resupplied with water enough to fill two canteens each, I took a salt tablet and drank one full canteen right away. I began to feel better in ten or fifteen minutes. After everybody had gotten their water, I went back to the pile of cans and tipped every one of them upside down. By collecting the last few drops of water that remained in each supply can, I was able to harvest almost a full canteen. I knew that when we got back to base, I would be finding additional canteens. We sat in for the night: established a perimeter, dug fighting holes, cut the tall grass from in front of the holes to improve lanes of fire and decrease the enemy's ability to sneak up on us. Then we ate a supper of C-rations and set a watch schedule.

One man in each position would be awake while the others slept. It was usually a three-hour shift per night, but that would change depending on the danger of the situation. A 50 percent alert meant two hours sleep and two hours awake through the night. Half the platoon was awake all night at these times. I took first watch, and when it ended, I was so tired that I didn't care about not having a bed. During the next couple of days, we swept through the area on a search and destroy mission with support from two or three tanks. Each day I became more acclimatized and stronger. Each night we repeated the process of setting in.

At one point we found a hidden cache of weapons, ammunition, and mortar rounds, which the engineers blew up with C4 plastic explosives. From the engineers, I got my first satchel bag, which was a green canvas bag about six inches wide, twelve inches long, and sixteen inches deep with a long web strap that stretched across my shoulder. The Unit One medical kit with a red cross on it was the first thing to go into this bag, along with extra battle dressings, gauze, and elastic bandages, thick glass bottles of intravenous (IV) fluids, and a large glass bottle of salt tablets. In time, I would have a satchel tied to each side of my backpack and one over each shoulder. We were eventually airlifted out to LZ Stud, which was the base I would come to think of as home when we were not out in the bush.

# LZ STUD

Landing Zone Stud, later known as Vandergrift Combat Base, was where we stood lines (we guarded the perimeter of the base from well-sandbagged and permanent bunkers.) It was our home when we were not out on combat missions. We alternated with the other companies in our battalion. We either stood lines or were out on missions.

I was in the 9th Marine Regiment, which consisted of three battalions called 1/9, 2/9, and 3/9. A battalion consisted of four companies labeled by letters and using phonetic names for each of those letters and also included a headquarters group and attached units such as supply, a mortar company, etc. So 1/9 had Alpha, Bravo, Charlie, and Delta companies. 2/9 had Echo, Foxtrot, Golf, and Hotel. 3/9 had India, Kilo, Lima, and Mike. I guess they skipped over J since no tough marine wanted to be in a company called Juliet.

Over the next three to four weeks, not much occurred in the way of combat. This gave me time to learn the day-to-day tasks of my job, such as keeping my pistol clean and becoming skilled at packing everything I needed in a very small backpack. I also learned how to keep things dry. This was not an easy trick when living in a tropical rain forest. It required many plastic bags. Daily patrols helped me gain physical strength and become better able to function in the heat and humidity.

I met our Battalion Surgeon, also known as Batt. Surg. He was a Navy Doctor named Pasker. He and the corpsmen manned and operated our Battalion Aide Station (BAS), which was very much like a combination doctor's office and emergency room in a tent. Doctor Pasker was my commanding officer, even though for most day-to-day matters and all things military, I was under the direction of the Marine officers and sergeants. When it came to things medical, I was responsible to Batt. Surg. and was basically in charge of all the health matters for the troops I was assigned to.

Every morning, I made my rounds with malaria pills and conversation. I soon came to know a lot about the young men that I would be caring for, living with, and entrusting with my own safety over the next few months. They were from all over the United States. They were farm boys and city kids, representing many creeds, religions, and colors. For all of us, this was a very unique situation, completely unlike anything we were used to. *The Old West must have been something like this*, I thought. Everyone you spoke with or saw was armed and, more often than not, under a great deal of personal stress. This was punctuated by the military's hurry-up-and-wait style of doing things. I cannot fully explain what it was like. The 2001 movie "Band of Brothers" comes very close to how we felt about each other. Friendships developed, some stronger than others. We were kindred spirits relying on each other as we faced the same adversities. My buddies were tough, well-trained fighters; many had been tested in battle. Inside each of us was also a scared half-grown kid, on the opposite side of the world from those people and places we knew and loved. We were depending on ourselves and each other to survive.

I learned a lot about trust and respect in Vietnam. Respect has to be earned, and it works best if it goes in both directions. I hope I earned respect in their eyes because I can say, without a single doubt, that these were the finest young men I've ever had the privilege of knowing. To this day, I would do anything they asked of me, if it was within my ability. It was and is a bond that is every bit as strong as a person has with family.

As I had promised myself out in the bush, one of the first things I did was to pick up two more canteens. I would eventually carry seven in all. I had four on my waist web belt and two tied to my backpack. The last one, inside the pack, would be for the wounded only. That was a promise I kept through my entire tour.

I maintained my 45 clean and in working order, and my K-Bar was sharp enough to shave with. I kept my socks dry and learned to tuck my trouser cuffs inside my boots to keep out the leeches. Because of the potential for jungle rot and other skin problems related to snug damp clothing rubbing and chafing skin, nobody wore underwear. Jungle utility uniforms were looser and did not chafe your skin, and the material dried out quickly. I also learned to play Back Alley Bridge and discovered that when dining on C-rations, the best dessert was peaches and pound cake, but they did not come in the same meal box so you had to choose carefully or trade to get both.

On payday, I would go to the small Base Exchange, literally a big steel box about the size of half a semi-truck trailer, and purchase writing paper and envelopes. I tried to write a letter every day to Harriet or my family. I was sure they would let each other know I had written. Mail from the United States had now caught up with me, and I can't tell you how much receiving letters meant to all of us. I was becoming acclimated to the heat and humidity and could now hike a long way carrying about one hundred pounds of equipment and not be totally exhausted.

The platoon moved as a unit, but every day, once we had picked a place to set in, one of the three squads would go out on a patrol and check out the area around our position. If we stayed in the same spot, there would be a morning and an afternoon patrol. A Marine would go out on every third patrol; a corpsman would go out on every other. After Doc Sieb got pulled back to the BAS, I went out on all of them. I was doing quite a bit of walking every day. Before Doc Sieb left, he told me that the usual rotation for a corpsman was six months in the bush, followed by six months in a BAS or one of the bigger units. Because the arrival of replacements had been at a high level recently, it was now more common to be pulled back after only four months. This was truly music to my ears. Over a month had passed, and while we had been on many patrols and missions, the worst injuries I had treated were minor cooking burns and occasional foot blisters. I would be thankful for the relative safety of the BAS, where I would have a dry bed in a tent, regular meals, and not have to stand watch in a hole. I was already one quarter of the way there. We had captured a lot of enemy food, weapons, and ammunition but actual contact with the enemy had been nonexistent. So far, this was like a big camping trip with food, water, and daily activities supplied by my Uncle Sam. I was even becoming a bit less fearful. *How quickly that would change.*

So far, our basic purpose was to go out and look for the North Vietnamese soldiers, also called "Charlie." I will just refer to them as the NVA so as to not confuse them with the name of our company. We would be airlifted by UH-46 Sea Knight helicopters to an area where enemy movement had been detected. We would then run patrols for three or four days trying to find them. This was called search and destroy. This concept of troop movement used air mobility for rapid movement of men in and out of a specific area. In a country like Vietnam where there were not many roads, it was much faster than using trucks or walking. We were also dealing with enemy forces that had been fighting for hundreds of years in this area. They had lots of time to construct underground tunnels and bunkers and bury supplies to be used later. We often found stashes of food, weapons, and ammo, which we destroyed. The tunnels and caves were not fancy. In most cases, they had been dug by hand into rock that was so hard that no timbers were needed for support. Holes were dug into and sometimes through mountains, literally by hand, which was amazing. This was the backyard of the enemy, and while we had a significant advantage in technology, the enemy had the advantage of knowing the area well. Many of the supplies had been carried in carts pulled by water buffalo or elephants, along mountain trails: more still on the backs of people, some of them were willing and some were slave labor. Our missions were to take away as many of these supplies as possible while not staying in the area long enough to allow a larger force to move in and attack us. After three or four days, we would pull back, and one of the other platoons would do a similar sweep in another area.

Highway 9 ran through the local towns of Cam Lo and Dong Ha, which was about as far south as I would be going until it was time for me to go home. Landing Zone Stud was located on Highway 9, south of Khe Sanh and north of Camp Carroll and Fire Base Rock Pile. When our missions were done, we would return to LZ Stud to rest, resupply, and stand perimeter guard. When Battalion Headquarters was moved here, LZ Stud was renamed Vandergrift Combat Base (VCB).

When we stood lines, we always had the same section of the perimeter. This covered about half a mile along the south side of the base. From Highway 9 at the eastern end, the line sloped gently down for one hundred yards or so. It then gradually climbed uphill the rest of the way. After going over the top of the hill, it curved around to the northwest and became another platoon's section. A well-worn, two-track road ran behind our position with a ridgeline just behind that. At the top of our hill, the positions were even with this ridge, but at our line's lowest point, it stood some thirty to forty feet above, at a forty-five degree slope. An Army Duster, which was a small armored vehicle with two fifty caliber guns mounted on top, was usually positioned on this ridge above and a little left of where I usually stayed. Sometimes, as night was setting in, the duster fired into the area in front of our bunker. If they were just covering the area to discourage any would-be attacker or if they had a specific target, I was never sure. Every fifth round was a tracer, so it was like having our own little fireworks display. In front of us stood three strands of barbed wire tangle foot strung eighteen inches apart and four to six inches high, low enough to prevent crawling under it and high enough to trip any running attacker, especially in the dark. Three coils of razor-edged wire, two at the bottom and one on top, stood about six to seven feet high and finished the defenses. We attached trip flares and old C-ration cans with pebbles inside to make a noise if the wire was disturbed. It was not a lot and would not stop a determined assault, but it would slow them down a bit. While considered meager protection by those who were stationed in Dong Ha or Quang Tri, we were happy to have anything between the enemy and us. We overlooked a wide flat valley of four-foot high grass, which extended for at least a "click," which is a thousand meters. That is about two and a half times around the quarter mile track that circles a football field. Beyond that, where the mountain began, were groves of thick bamboo.

The bunker was located in the middle of our section of the perimeter. I usually stayed the night there with three men. Gene, a tall and lanky kid from Munsey, Indiana, was the team leader. Chuck had olive skin and black hair, and although short in stature, he could hump all his gear and four cans of machine gun ammo all day. Mike was a tall and lanky California dude. They made up one of our M60 machine gun teams. Staying with them, I was at an equal distance from both ends of the area I had to cover.

We had a ten-by-ten foot bunker with a steel roof. Standing up inside, I could easily see or shoot through foot-high openings created by the removal of sandbags. The above-ground part, about eighteen inches, of this structure was surrounded by sandbags, three or four thick, while the roof had six layers. If it rained, I could sleep inside the bunker for shelter. On dry nights, I had my quarters set up along the outside wall. I had scrounged two eight-foot-long steel fence posts that I threaded through the side pockets of my nylon stretcher. The four corners were then set on stacks of sandbags, which would keep my bed a foot and a half off the ground, and a couple more sandbags on top of the poles held it in place. With six-foot poles, I made a large X at each end of the bed and ran a rope over the cross braces and staked it. Finally, I draped my poncho over the rope and staked its sides to form a one-man pup tent. A piece of C-ration cardboard protected the ends from weather. In this way, my gear stayed up off the ground and dry or under my bed and out of the dew when I was sleeping at night.

The most amazing thing we had at this bunker was Ricky Ticky, a mongoose. Yes, he was the furry little weasel-like animal, who lived about eight to twelve feet in front of and to the right of the bunker. We would toss him scraps of food, and he, in return, kept the snakes away. We always left a note at the bunker when we went out on an operation; that way, whoever took over our spot would be able to keep Ricky Ticky happy. He was never domesticated, but I always slept better knowing he was on patrol.

## FIRST SERIOUS HOUSE CALL

Sometime in late August or early September, when we were putting our gear in the bunker, a big storm began moving up the valley. I was in the bunker when the rain started to fall. I heard a loud crackle followed by a boom. It was close. It did not sound at all like incoming fire, but I called down the line to check for injuries.

"Hey, Doc!" came a voice from the next hole. "A bolt of lightning just hit the Duster."

Not knowing what I would find, I grabbed my medical bag and took off up the hill. As I approached the top, two men staggered out of the vehicle. They had been shutting equipment down inside when the lightning struck their whip antenna. Making them sit down before they fell, I began to assess and treat them. Several of my buddies arrived to help, and word reached our radioman to call for a med evac. In this case, a jeep from BAS would do just fine. The two wounded soldiers had suffered burns and scrambled nervous systems, but their heartbeats and respirations were stable. This was a miracle. We wrapped them in poncho liners, and soon the jeep arrived with a doctor. We got them loaded on the jeep and down to BAS for further treatment. They were flown to a larger facility with more diagnostic capability. Like most of the men I cared for, I never did find out what happened to them. I am relatively sure that they recovered. So my first real casualties were Army and not combat related.

From here on, the sequence of events may be a bit out of order. Things were about to get a whole lot more intense. I still remember the events, but after forty years the sequences are not always clear. My mind still tries to protect me.

## COMBAT RADIO

Now would be a good time for a brief lesson in radio protocol. We used the standard phonetic alphabet, where each letter was given a word that begins with that letter. Much of the same code is used today. It is widely known so no secrets are being revealed. You have already seen some of its usage in company names. Doc Sieb was moved back to BAS and the Headquarters group and became senior squid, and for a long time, I was the only corpsman in the platoon. On the radio, we did not use real names because the enemy might be listening. Since the troops called me either Doc John or Squid, my radio call sign became "Charlie Two Squid." This was derived from my company, platoon, and my being Navy. We used either a number or letter so that communications would be clear as to the talker and the listener. "Charlie Two Romeo Oscar" was C Company Second Platoon, radio operator. "Charlie Two Three Lima Papa" was the Third Squad out on a listening post. "Tell character November Alpha Victor Yankee type Juliet Hotel his test results just came back and he is Echo Four" meant to let your Navy person John Holm know he got promoted to enlisted pay grade four.

It seemed that everyone had a letter and/or number sign. For example, "Charlie Six Actual" was the company commander, while "Charlie Two Six Actual" was the second platoon commander. While confusing at first, it soon became a very clear and effective way to communicate. Like all occupations, soldiering has its own vocabulary. You also never said "repeat" on the radio, which was only used for fire missions. The proper response if you did not hear something clearly was "Say again." When you were finished with a statement and awaiting a response, you signified by saying over. When you were finished with the conversation, you signified by saying out. This should help you to understand some of the dialogue later on.

## IT HAD HIT THE FAN IN LEATHERNECK SQUARE

It was not too long before we received our next mission. Bravo Company was out in an area called Leatherneck Square. They had contact with the NVA and had taken heavy casualties. Somebody somewhere, in his infinite wisdom and with a grossly inflated opinion of just how tough Marines are, sent Second Platoon Charlie Company up to bail them out. The UH-46 Sea Knight helicopters sat us down on a ridgeline facing a much bigger, much higher ridge. It was really your basic mountain. As we exited and fanned out to reinforce the position, the wounded were loaded for evacuation first and then the dead. Our first task involved following a footpath to where one of Bravo's squads had been badly mauled. I knew we were walking right into the enemy area and were carefully checking each of the bodies we came to, while staying alert for an ambush. We were providing security so that the Bravo guys could remove the bodies of their Killed-In-Action. I heard one of my buddies say, "Sarge! I have movement down here. Can I shoot?"

"Hell, no. They're being good enough to let us have our dead," the sergeant replied.

This was one of several times that I observed that there still could be honor on the field of battle.

We had Phantom jets flying support and making bomb runs on the mountain during this time. I had no idea how big a force we were up against, but as the jets came in on their runs, they were taking fire from NVA machine guns. That does not happen unless it's a very large number of troops or the gunners are chained to their weapons and unable to hide.

I knew we were being observed because as soon as we loaded out the last of our wounded and dead, we started taking incoming fire from mortars. I remember thinking that only the Marine Corps could come up with a plan that goes: If a company gets waxed by a battalion or regiment of NVA, let's send up a platoon from Charlie Company to even the odds. We may have been good, but come on!

So now with mortar rounds exploding all around us, my office hours got longer. This was my first time doing my job while under attack, and words cannot describe how scary this was as I moved from man to man. With the adrenaline in my body pumping sky-high, I felt like a spectator watching my own hands do their job. But all of my training back on the grinder at Camp Pendleton worked, and now I found out how I would behave in combat.

With four or five of my guys wounded, F4 Phantom jets screaming overhead, Sea Knights coming in to take us out, no one to shoot back at, and mortar rounds exploding everywhere, I was out there running from man to man, and now we were beginning to take rifle fire. Talk about not having the sense to come in from the rain. This was not fun. When there were no more wounded to treat, I crouched down in a foxhole about thirty yards from the LZ awaiting the next call for "Squid up!" My mouth was like cotton, and all my water was gone. I was up to carrying four canteens now, all of them empty. I needed to carry more. I opened the only liquid I had, a bottle of plasma expander. I tried a sip. It was terrible.

By now, there were only about a dozen of us left on the ridge. As the Sea Knight landed, the men ran toward the back ramp of the helicopter. I heard the distinctive *bloop, bloop* sound of mortars being fired.

"Tubes popping," someone shouted.

The helicopter lifted off, the men pulled back, and two explosions occurred right where they had been. This happened two more times, and I watched as Marines moved toward and then away from the helicopter like waves on a beach. I was sitting in this hole in the ground thinking, *it's a lot safer than being out there*. Right about now, the Forward Observer (FO) and his Radio Telephone Operator (RTO) came running up the trail and past my position, and it hit me that this was probably the last bus leaving this station today. Yeah, I know, real corny, but that is what ran through my mind at that instant. I got up out of the hole and was right behind them as the helicopter sat down again. Everyone else was on board as the three of us got there. The FO was up the ramp; his radioman slipped on the ramp in front of me, blocking my way, so with one hand I grabbed a piece of helicopter and with the other I grabbed him by the belt and threw him the rest of the way in. I do not know if it was the rear of the helicopter lifting up or the blast from the mortar round that impacted behind us, but I landed rather unceremoniously face first on the floor of the helicopter.

Doing a quick inventory of all my body parts and not feeling any pain, I sat up and flipped the bird back to where we had just been. One of the marines had lit a cigarette and handed it to me. As I passed it back, I noticed a spot of blood on it and discovered that I had split my lip on my less-than-graceful boarding of the aircraft. Well, I had now shed blood for my country and was very grateful it was only due to my own clumsiness.

When we landed back at Vandergrift, I drank three full canteens of water from the first water bull, I found. The thing looked like a small railroad tank car pulled by a jeep or truck and held a lot of water. Then up to Battalion Aide Station to replenish my supplies and have the doctor make sure my lip was okay. It was.

## SEARCH AND DESTROY

For the next couple of months, we alternated between standing guard at VCB and running sweep-and-destroy missions in the Kentucky, Scotland, Lancaster, and Trousdale areas. I wondered who I needed to see to get the job where I could sit in an air conditioned tent and give arbitrary names to places. We captured a large quantity of NVA supplies that had been hidden in caves and bunkers. The combat engineers blew up the weapons, battle gear, and ammunition while the food was airlifted out and distributed to people displaced by the fighting and now living in refugee camps.

Often we made contact with NVA units, and there would be a brief gun battle (also called a firefight) or mortar attack. The call, "Tubes popping!" sent us all running for cover.

The sound made by a mortar being fired was a distinctive *bloop* and always occurred a few seconds before the explosion of the round's impact. You could never tell where a round would hit, but you did know that very soon the airspace, waist-high and above, was going to be filled with fast-moving pieces of hot metal and rocks.

I kept very busy honing my medical skills and learning the other lessons I would need to keep me alive in the bush. One of the skills that I developed was the ability to run rapidly in a crouched position; another was to quickly evaluate and then use every bit of cover available to me. The NVA could shoot me if they did not see me. Most of the time I do not think that even my own men saw my comings and goings.

## TEST DAY

It started out as a routine day in September. We were standing lines at Vandergrift when I received a radio message from BAS telling me to catch a helicopter ride back to Quang Tri. I was scheduled to take my test for advancement. My first thoughts were, "Why do I have to take a written test in a combat zone?" I was doing my job well, and I surely had no time to study, and I still had to take a stupid test? I will forever be amazed by the infinite wisdom of the military.

At least this would mean a hot cooked meal instead of C-rations and a chance to go to my seabag for some writing paper and extra socks. Back in Quang Tri, I unloaded my 45 and, for the first time in a couple of months, felt relatively safe. I wrote my test, had a good meal at the mess hall, collected my extras, and flew back to Vandergrift before dark. It was a nice break, and I felt pretty good about my answers on the test.

A few weeks later, in early October, I received another message that I had passed the test. My promotion was approved.

I was now an (E4) Hospital Corpsman Third Class, which did not change my job any, but just gave me a raise in pay. I was now earning $14.07 a day. My buddies had a good time tacking on my new stripe. Tradition is, each man punched my upper arm where the new insignia goes on, which makes for a somewhat sore arm for a couple of days.

## STATE FLAG

Several of the men had brought their home state flags, which they flew when we were back at Vandergrift. I quickly noticed that Michigan was not among them. *This would not do*, I thought. To correct this omission, I wrote a letter to Governor George Romney. Why not go straight to the top? I explained my situation and asked if it would be possible to obtain a Michigan state flag.

It was not too long before I received his answer. At mail call, I received a package with a Lansing, Michigan return address. My state flag now proudly joined the others, waving in the hot breezes that blew through the compound.

# ADVENTURES IN DMZNEYLAND

While we often went out as a platoon-sized force on our missions, there were times when the situation required a larger response. Such was the case when the whole 1st Battalion was assigned to go into the demilitarized zone (DMZ). Intelligence reports had spotted a North Vietnamese base camp in the DMZ. They had broken the rules by establishing a forward base so close, and to leave this move unchallenged would have made our situation increasingly dangerous. The plan was to go in fast, hit them hard, and be back at VCB in three days. The orders were: pack light, no extra clothing or shaving gear needed, just three days' food, and battle gear. For me, that meant extra dressing supplies and IV fluids. The weight saved on personal gear was more than offset by packing extra ammo and mortar rounds. By now, I had trained all the men in my care to carry one small battle dressing in their right shirt pocket and another in their helmet band. I had also taught them the proper way to apply one. This allowed more room in my supplies for the medium and large dressings, which gave me a working supply of about one hundred. My rule was that if a man was wounded, I would use the dressings he carried first.

"They weigh less than an ounce. Do not throw them away," I said repeatedly.

My food rations on this mission included a pint jar of venison that my mother had canned and sent from home. My father, an avid bow hunter, had harvested the deer a few weeks earlier. Because of my blond hair and blue eyes, many people were unaware of my Potawatomi roots. This was my kind of meal. The venison would last for three or more meals.

It was the biggest troop movement I had seen until now. All four companies, the Headquarters group, and an attached Mortar Company were lined up along both sides of the landing strip. Six Sea Knights would set down, take on troops, and lift off as the next wave of six came in. We were soon all airborne and headed north. They inserted us on several different mountaintop

45

LZs surrounding the suspected enemy base camp. We quickly disembarked and took up defensive positions to protect the landing zone, while I paid close attention to where each and every Marine was positioned. I also located the available cover in the area in case I needed it.

I had looked at the map before we left, and I knew what the area should look like. When we landed, however, things just did not look right to me. I scurried over to Gene and got out a map and compass. Before long, I figured out that we were not where I had been told we would be. We were on the north side of the Ben Ha River. I was sure somebody had made a mistake. *Things are not going to be good*, I thought. However, I did not have time to worry since we immediately got organized and moved southeast off the LZ. We went down the mountain, crossed the river, and started back uphill on the South Vietnamese side. Crossing the river, I pulled the camera and state flag from my pack and, standing on a large boulder in the middle, had one of the guys take my picture on the border of the two countries.

About an hour later, we were moving up the mountain when an explosion ripped the air thirty to forty yards ahead. The Marines all dropped to the ground, assuming their alternate facing defensive positions. I was already moving forward toward the spot of the blast, when I heard, "Corpsman up!"

I picked up my pace and quickly got to the downed men; both of them were dead. One had been a new replacement who had joined us just prior to the operation. He had apparently watched too many gung ho war movies because he had tied his hand grenades, through the pins, to his flak jacket. While walking through the chin-high scrub brush, the grenades caught on the limbs and pulled off. Ten seconds later, he and another man lay dead on the mountainside. It is never easy to lose a fellow Marine, but this experience was especially tragic. The second victim, Robinson, had only two weeks left in country. To survive fifty weeks of your tour of duty only to be taken out by a stupid accident made us all feel vulnerable. Two others received very minor Band-Aid wounds, which I took care of right away. We called for dust-off, evacuation by helicopter, to pick up the two that did not make it, and continued our assault up the north side of the mountain.

By midafternoon, we found ourselves, along with the other companies, in the middle of an abandoned North Vietnamese Army encampment. Hoping to entrap the NVA, each company had come up a different side of the mountain. They must have received word that we were coming and had moved out. It had been a major base. The shelters, complete with tables and chairs, had been roofed with foliage. Privies had been dug and well used. We had only missed them by one or two days. The intelligence guys collected the few scraps that were left behind.

We sat up our defenses for the night, grateful that we had not had to fight our way in. A lot more folks would have gotten hurt. The next morning, the helicopters arrived, taking out the headquarters and intelligence types and dropping off engineers with chainsaws and C4 plastic explosives. For the next couple of weeks, we walked out of the DMZ, each of the four companies taking a different route. Our jobs were to clear landing zones on just about every mountaintop along the way. On more than one occasion, while listening to the buzzing of chainsaws, the perimeter watch would shout, "Tubes popping!"

Everyone would seek shelter in the safest place they could find. I usually crawled under a downed tree trunk. Although a few mortar rounds would land and explode near us, usually no one was injured. We would then go back to work until the next alert. About every third day, I would have to evacuate somebody with shrapnel wounds that were serious but not life-threatening. I think most went directly to one of our hospital ships, the *USS Sanctuary* or *USS Repose*, alternately stationed just off the coast.

Eventually, we made it far enough south and managed to clear enough mountaintops to make the brass happy. They finally sent helicopters to take us back to VCB. We had been almost a month in the heat and humidity without a bath or shave. You may recall my saying that we packed very light going out. By this time, several of us had very unmilitary-like scruffy faces.

As we walked down to the river for a bath, several of us were fantasizing what it would be like if, all of a sudden, the war ended and we were put on a plane and flown into a state side airport. We figured we would probably remain in our current uncivilized mind-set so some of the suggestions included setting up a command post near the water cooler, while the M-60 teams covered the escalators. It would be critical to secure the vending machines as a supply source. I assured them that right now our best defense was our appearance. We looked and smelled so bad that no one would come near us. In my current condition, I even found myself offensive to be around. After washing out our clothing and bathing in the river, we walked back up the hill to mail call. Letters from the world kept us going, informed us of what was happening with our families and friends and, for a time, drove away the fear. After such a long mission, there were also "care packages." These were boxes sent by our families containing powdered drinks and soups, Jiffy Popcorn, books, and homemade treats; my favorite was chocolate chip cookies. Most of the time, they arrived as a box or tin of crumbs, but I can tell you every spoonful tasted wonderful.

# MAP READING: HOW AND WHY

I guess a word or two about map reading would be a helpful thing to know. Wherever we went, we always had good topographical maps of the area. Those are maps with all the little squiggly circles on them representing the distance above sea level; each circle meant fifty or a hundred meters higher, depending on the scale. Where the lines were further apart, the slope of the land was gentler and, if they were very close together, it was steep. From top to bottom and side to side, grid lines were drawn and numbered at every one thousand meters, also known as one click, so each grid square had two numbers, one vertical and one horizontal. With a bit of experience, a good view, and a compass, you could always tell another person with the same map exactly where you were. This is very important information if you needed a dust-off, aircraft or artillery fire support, supplies in a hurry, or simply to be rescued.

One meter is about three inches longer than a yardstick. Since a thousand square meters is a relatively big space, halfway between grid lines sixteen and seventeen was coordinate 1650, three quarters between lines eleven and twelve would be 1175 and so forth. So by giving a ship off the coast or an artillery battery ten miles away, the right map number, and the right coordinates, they could shoot their big guns and hit where you asked them to. As long as you knew where you were, the map numbers that you both had were correct, and they did their math right, the incoming shells would land on the enemy and not on you. If anyone got their numbers wrong, things could get real dicey, real fast. Many people died from "friendly fire," and while that sounds like a contradiction in terms, it did happen.

We often had a Forward Observer (FO) and his Radio Telephone Operator (RTO) attached to us to do this job. In the absence of an FO, any of us, even the corpsman, was able to do this job. When time allowed, we would call for one or two "spotter rounds." These were white phosphorus called "Willy Pete," and when one exploded, there was a lot of white smoke.

They were less destructive but still dangerous, if you were too close. After seeing where the round landed, we could make an adjustment if necessary.

"Aim two hundred left, and one hundred up, and fire for effect!"

The rounds after the spotting shells were called Heat (high explosive). They would usually fire about ten rounds into the target. If the enemy was still shooting, we could make further adjustments or hit the same area with more, with the command, "Repeat!"

For air support, we might be lucky to have an Aerial Observer (AO) in a lightweight plane covering us. He could fly slowly, actually see the enemy, and carried mostly Willie Pete rockets, which, when fired into the target area, would leave a big cloud of white smoke. The jets would then drop their bombs in the designated spot. When we did not have the luxury of an AO, we carried different colored smoke grenades and, once the plane or helicopters were overhead, we could radio them the color of the smoke cloud we threw, the direction, and the distance to the target. We had to be in radio contact with the aircraft because the enemy carried smoke too and could cause confusion for the pilots. These same procedures were used to call in a dust-off or supply helicopter. As you can see, the ability to read a map well could be very important for more things than finding a good route from point A to point B.

## DAILY BUSINESS OR THIS IS WAR

Back in the camp, a lot was happening on a daily basis. New men arrived to replace the dead, wounded, and those rotating home. Some of the men were nearing the end of their tours, "getting short." They would be going back to The World soon. It never seemed that the arrivals equaled the number of departures. We always seemed to be slightly below our full strength.

It was discovered that Lieutenant Casey was the sole male heir to the family name, and because of the Sullivan Act, he was on his way home early. He had been a high school Math teacher in civilian life and was a great guy and good leader. Lieutenant Webster, a lanky Texan, was his replacement. We were grateful that he was equal to Lieutenant Casey in his concern for the men and doing his job well. His educational background was in geology. Many times, as we moved through the bush, I would see an unusual rock formation and ask questions about the land around us. He would explain to me the significance of the rock formations and composition of the soil. I felt that he was happy to think about something other than the war for a few minutes. His tactical skills were top-notch, he treated all the men fairly, and he stood up for us when needed.

Sergeant Christensen also joined us during this time. I really liked him for his common sense, courage, and the advice he gave. One of his wonderful quirks was waking in the morning and promptly shouting out, "If it's green, it's good!"

He may have seen too many Marine Corps training films.

I had many duties back at base, such as the daily pill/sick call rounds, writing letters, keeping up with our running card games, giving haircuts (for some unknown reason, I was carrying the one set of hair clippers we had in the platoon), and feeding Ricky Ticky the mongoose. I was also the sanitation officer for the platoon.

Out in the bush, when you needed to relieve yourself, you could go behind a tree or dig a small "cat hole" in the ground. A small quantity of toilet paper came in each box of C-rations. In a contained and frequently lived-in setting, this practice would very soon make for a very smelly and bacteria-prone living space, where disease would be a real danger, so designated places were established as bathrooms. For the more simple function of urinating, a good-sized hole, about four to five feet deep, was dug in the ground. It was then backfilled with crushed rock or gravel. A length of five-inch diameter tile pipe was set in and the hole was covered with dirt, leaving the pipe sticking up from the ground two feet and at a forty-five degree angle. These were placed behind the lines every hundred yards or so, and provided your aim was reasonably good, they served their purpose quite well. They were basically freestanding septic tanks.

Let me describe a standard issue military privy or outhouse: Start with a wooden box, three feet tall by three feet wide; the length can vary depending on the seating capacity desired. On top of this, build a rectangular shelter with room to walk in and sit down. The bottom three quarters of the walls are boarded for privacy, and the top portion is screened up to the slanted roof for ventilation. Put a door at each end. Inside this large outhouse, on the top surface of the box, cut fanny-sized holes. In our case, it was a four-seater. Insert a peg for holding a roll of toilet paper in front of each hole. Place half of a fifty-five gallon steel barrel beneath each hole.

The outside of the original box was top-hinged, on the back, so that you could lift it up, prop it with a stick, and gain access to these oversized chamber pots.

"Why would anyone want to do that?" a sensible person might ask.

I will tell you why. The engineers had made a handle hole on either side of the barrels so you could use a pole to remove them, and when a barrel was a bit over half full, it needed to be pulled out and replaced with an empty one. All right, full out and empty in, now what? Move them away from the outhouse a few yards and stack them in a pyramid. Next, take a big stick, some JP-4 (aviation gas) and fuel oil, stir until mixed well, and finally add a match. I always tried to do this job on days when the wind was blowing away from the camp and usually volunteered two men to help me. I could have assigned this rather unpleasant task to others, but since I did not like to ask anyone to do something I wouldn't do myself, I usually worked with them. Once the fire had burned itself out, the only thing left was an inch of ashes with absolutely no resemblance to the original material, which was then dumped in a pit dug for that purpose and you were left with empty barrels for next time. Now that the question has been answered about where the empties came from and you are probably completely grossed out, just remember, we had a saying in the 1960s. Shit happens!

## ANIMAL LIFE

Maybe now would be as good a time as any to discuss the animals that inhabited this area since they were not only a part of my stories but also a part of my fears. I have already mentioned our mongoose friend. One of the mainstays of his diet was snakes, so he goes on the list of good guys. Elephants, both domesticated and wild, lived in these mountains. Tigers were among the critters that caused concern, and I had a close encounter with one that I will tell more about later. Rock apes were a relatively small member of the ape family and were very curious. They lived on the sides of mountains, the steeper the better, because that was their protection from predators. They also defended their territory by throwing things down on anything or anyone they felt was too close. Things thrown usually consisted of sticks, poop, and stones. You definitely did not want to throw a hand grenade at them because they would toss it right back.

There was a small species of the deer family, which, like most deer, was relatively timid. Unless you moved very quietly, they were gone before you saw them. Monkeys of several varieties lived in the lush canopy of the jungle treetops, along with an incredible number of birds in all the colors of the rainbow. Insects were everywhere, and my least favorite was the fiercely aggressive mosquito. Though not technically insects, there were at least two distinct kinds of leeches. The flat, black ones that lived in the water looked a lot like those found in the rivers and streams back home, except that these were up to five inches long. The ones we called elephant leeches lived on dry land. They were about one and a half inches long, a light gray-green color, and shaped like small baseball bats, until they fed on you. Then they became about as big as a thumb and tapered at both ends. In a partially effective attempt to keep them off our skin, we kept the bottom cuff of our trousers tied and tucked into our boots. The only difference between the feeling of a drop of perspiration on your back and a leech was that the sweat ran downward.

One morning, I awoke and felt that very soft sliding on my left shoulder. Quickly pulling my shirt back, I found the offender. There was a small amount of clotted blood on my left cheek, and he was very bloated after dining on me. I was the last meal that one ever had.

There were many kinds of snakes. The two that were most plentiful and troublesome were the cobras and bamboo vipers. You, of course, have seen pictures of the cobras with their hoods flared. Believe me, they look even more frightening up close and in person. The bamboo viper was smaller; the biggest one I saw was a couple of feet long and thinner than a broom handle. But the venom is highly toxic. Their injecting fangs were at the back of their jaws, so they had to bite you someplace narrow, like the webbing between the fingers or on your earlobes. The standard statement was that a bamboo viper had to chew on you some. The front half of their body was dark bamboo green, which faded to new growth green toward the tails so they would blend into bamboo thickets perfectly. I feared these the most because if they were to bite someone, there was not much I could do to stop the neurotoxic venom. With my entrenching tool, I whacked the head off whenever I found one. Due to the inherent danger of this activity, I was discouraged from doing so.

There were also rats, mice, and an abundance of other small rodents. Except for the occasional rat bite, no other problems were caused.

In the villages were the usual domestic animals such as pigs (the pot-bellied type), chickens, ducks, goats, water buffalo (they could be a rather surly lot), and the occasional dog (sandy reddish-colored, they looked like a relative of the dingo species). All of the above could be on the lunch or dinner menu. The water buffalo, the animal not the water trailer, usually gray in color, looks much more like a cow than a buffalo. They weighed about half a ton, give or take a hundred pounds, and took the place of a farmer's tractor.

The Marine Corps also had scout dogs. They went out on missions with us from time to time. I remember two of them; one was a silver-gray German Shepherd, whose name I do not recall. What I do remember most about her was that she disliked all Vietnamese people. She would snarl and bare her teeth, whether they were from the north or south. She was almost as intolerant of Black American troops and only tolerated the rest of us during the daylight. I was certain that at night she would have attacked anyone who came within a ten- to twenty-yard range. What was obvious to me was that if her handler were ever wounded and unable to talk, I would probably have to shoot the dog before I could care for him. As often as I tried to make her comfortable around me, she never did warm up. Her handler also made it clear that he did not want me to establish any relationship with him or the dog. He was a loner and made it an obvious point to eat and sleep in an area away from the rest of us.

The other scout dog was a big black and tan German Shepherd named Hobo. He worked with us frequently. First and foremost, he was probably the most handsome and fit German Shepherd I had ever seen, and I soon learned that he outranked me! He carried the rank of Captain in the scout dog corps. Ron, Hobo's handler, was an easygoing guy from Pennsylvania. He understood that the time might come when he would potentially need my help and did not discourage my overtures of friendship. I frequently would sit down with Ron and Hobo to talk or eat. Hobo sat on the opposite side of Ron, keeping a close watch. Soon, he relaxed when I came around and would come around and sniff my knee or hand. My patience paid off, and he decided I was not a threat. He would even let me pet him and shake hands. This would prove to be a very good thing, as you will see when I tell more about Hobo later.

NOT SO SECRET WEAPON—Pfc. Ronald T. Boone guides his scout dog, Hobo, as
they track down the elusive enemy. Credited with saving many American lives since
they became a team in May 1968, the two are members of Scout Dog Platoon, 3rd
Military Police Bn., FLC.
(Photo by Cpl. John S. Krill)

# WELL ARMED

After a short stay on the *USS Repose*, one of the first casualties I
had patched up in Leatherneck Square returned and was assigned
the job of handing out weapons at the armory. For the rest of
my time in the country, all I needed to do was to walk over to
the armory tent and tell him what I wanted to carry on our next
mission. For a while, I carried a 45 caliber machine gun called a
grease gun. It was a dull silver color and resembled a large tin can
with a five-inch piece of pipe in front, a pistol grip, a trigger, and
a small rectangular bracket that held the fifty-round clip on the
underside. Ugly but dependable, the biggest drawbacks were the
volume and weight of the bullets. On other missions, I carried a
30-06 sniper's rifle with a scope, an M-16, an AR-15, a 12-gauge

pump shotgun, or an M-79 grenade launcher (called a Blooper). I always carried my Colt M-1911, a 45 caliber pistol. For the most part, carrying them was all I did since when a firefight started, I was busy doing my job. I had little time for shooting at anything. The main thing I accomplished was that, from a distance, I did not look at all like a corpsman.

## FIREBASE ANN

Our next mission was to Hill 950, so named because it was nine hundred and fifty meters above sea level. I guess the guy back in the rear had not yet come up with a catchy name for it yet. Hill 950 was a radio relay station overlooking the Khe Sanh Valley, but the mission first took us to Firebase Ann. We stayed at Ann for about three days because of thick clouds, which made landing a helicopter impossible. At first, the weather closed in on 950, then it settled on Ann. We kept busy running patrols during the day and setting up listening posts and/or ambushes at night. A listening post was three to four men positioned about fifty yards in front of the night perimeter. Their job was to listen for the enemy trying to sneak up on us and provide an early warning. An ambush was more men and could involve a whole platoon. They would set up in the best tactical position for the area, such as flanking both sides of a trail. Their job was to kill the enemy. Unless the ambush was platoon-sized or larger, the corpsman did not usually go. We had both an ambush and listening post out one of these nights and, due to fewer people being available to cover the fighting positions, I found myself standing a line watch. Adding me to the foxhole meant we could set a three-person watch schedule, which would enable all of us to get a little more sleep that Saturday night. It also resulted in my not being on a radio watch so I was unaware that our listening post had reported a tiger in the area.

## OUT OF THE MIST

It was early on Sunday morning and I was making my way from one foxhole to the next, dispensing the weekly orange malaria pills. The clouds had settled in on us so thick that I could only see about six feet in any direction. Things seemed calm; I had stood line watch the night before, not my usual radio watch at the command post, and was not aware of any threats in the area. I was tired and wanted to get my job done quickly. So I got to thinking I could move more quickly with just my med kit and K-Bar.

For a while, my task dragged on, mundane and uneventful. I would hand over the pills, stand and watch as the pill, amidst curses and grumbling, was thrown down the throat of the recipient. I was midway through my task when I began to notice that the fog was growing even more dense, and visibility was decreasing by the minute. Although I was still within earshot of the next position, I could see no one. I shivered as a feeling of uneasiness enveloped my being. I had been spooked. I did my best to shake it off and kept walking. At some point, the boogeymen were beginning to overwhelm my thoughts, and I paused to gather my bearings.

I have never been a man intimidated by the elements. I have hunted with my father and grandfather many times in Michigan and navigated successfully in dense fog and blinding blankets of snow. But that morning in Vietnam, the fog seemed to hold a kind of danger different from any that I had ever encountered. In a very short period of time, every warning system in my body was going off. I did my best to steady myself, took a few deep breaths and told myself that the situation was under control, and kept moving cautiously forward. Whatever this was, I had to do my best to get through it. I am, and was then, a rational guy, not prone to having my imagination get the better of me. Using all my senses, I was evaluating what was occurring when a strange feral smell crossed my path. I froze. Something was out there. From a place that I could not see came a low guttural rumble. I did not know what it was, but at that moment the sound of an AK-47 would have been less frightening. I stopped breathing. Moving only my eyes, I scanned my surroundings and had an eerie foreboding in my chest. Enshrouded in fog as I was, I knew that something knew exactly where I was. I understood that I could not have been a more vibrant target had I worn a flashing neon sign on my helmet. I unsheathed my K-Bar. All I could do was stand there and wait. So that is what I did.

I do not recall how long I stood there. It could have been a moment, or it could have been much longer. I can still see myself, frozen in place, transfixed by the image of a figure slowly taking form in the mist before me. *This might be where I die, but not easily*, I thought. The form materialized, and I heard the familiar voice of a Marine, "Doc! Where is your rifle?"

He must have thought I had been struck dumb, my only response being a solitary exhalation of breath.

"There is a tiger in the area," he told me. "I'll go with you to finish your rounds."

Still too stunned to respond and too relieved to protest, I followed this fellow Marine and buddy, who had saved me from something very lethal or perhaps from my own imagination, and I finished dispensing my big orange pills.

To this day, I do not know what, if anything, was lying in wait for me in that foggy jungle. Perhaps it was an animal that was tired of the intruders in his world, or maybe it was merely the conjurings of a tired and exhausted mind. I will never know the answer to that question. I do know that this was the day when I realized that in Vietnam, the enemies were not always wearing the red insignia of the NVA. Many things can come at a person out of the mist.

## HILL 950/ WHO IS PIG PEN?

The weather finally cleared at both sites, so we saddled up and the UH-46s came in and carried us up to 950. Looking out the window at the small platform that was our LZ was not encouraging, and what made things worse was the sight of a broken UH-46 Sea Knight that lay on its side in the wires just a few yards from where we had hoped to land. It had been immediately ahead of us and, through either an engine failure or an updraft, had flipped and crashed. We landed safely and took up our positions. I quickly checked to see if anyone had been hurt on the downed helicopter. Thankfully, all had walked away with only bumps and bruises. Any landing you can walk away from is a good landing.

The whole base on 950 would have fit inside a football field, without reaching either goal line. It was a radio relay station, which made it a single platoon-sized garrison. An Army unit under the command of some first lieutenant, whose daddy was a general, had manned it before us and had trashed the place. With the help of the combat engineers, our job was to strengthen the fortifications and clean up the place. A ring of sandbags, three bags thick and four to five feet tall, circled the top of the hill. Who were they kidding? This was your basic mountain! Outside the sandbag wall, for about forty feet, were concentric circles of three-strand barbed wire fences, tangle foot, and coiled razor wire, all of which was set on top of a minefield. As an added surprise, the map of the minefield had been lost so we had no clue where the mines were. The previous tenants had just tossed their empty and half-eaten C-ration cans into the wire so that the whole area looked and smelled like the rat-infested dump it was.

The combat engineers, the guys who really liked to play with things that go boom, would push Bangalore Torpedoes, tubes of plastic explosive, eight feet long and two inches in diameter, under the wire and trash. The design of these tubes allowed them to be joined, end-to-end, so that by adding a section at a time and advancing it another length, they eventually stuck out forty feet. The trick was to not hit any mines while pushing them out there. When they had repeated this process until they had three to five rows, six to eight feet apart, they would attach blasting caps and a fuse and shout, "Fire in the hole!"

We would all move to cover just before detonation. This exploded hidden mines and threw trash, barbed wire, and rats over the edge of the mountain. Come to think of it, this also created another area of tough going for any one attempting to climb up to attack us. It was tough going for the rats because after each section was cleared, you would see the survivors staggering from small piles that clung to the more sturdy posts, heading for the constantly shrinking area that had yet to be cleared. When the engineers finished clearing all the existing defenses, we would be replacing them with new ones. Until then, we kept busy sandbagging the roofs and walls of the bunkers and running daily patrols.

There was a time when the enemy had made an attempt to tunnel into this base without success. Knowing that little piece of history prompted us to do daily patrols around the top of 950 and across a saddle over to 1015, another hill/mountain named for its height. It was just a little under a click away. 1015 was a potential spot for a mortar to be set up and fired on us, so we needed to keep it clear. The perimeter sweeps were to prevent another tunneling attempt. These were difficult only because of the steepness of the slope. We did not encounter any major resistance while staying on the high ground, but patrols that went further down into the valley to fill canteens from a stream were often ambushed. We knew that we had to stay alert. I really hated sitting in one spot for so long because it took away our ability to use the element of surprise. It allowed the NVA time to move in on us.

The bunkers up on 950 were great quarters, approximately twelve feet by twelve feet and made from timbers having the thickness of railroad ties, with steel runway matting for roofs. They were reinforced with sandbags, about four to five thick, all the way around. They could have taken a hit from a mortar round or rocket-propelled grenade (RPG), and while the occupants may have gotten headaches, they would have survived. Along three walls were built-in bunks, three high, and along the fourth wall were a makeshift table, a chair, and the door. The really great part about them was that they were completely enclosed so at night I could sit at the desk and write letters or read by the light of my homemade lamp. The base of this lamp was a tin can about the size of a soup can. It contained fuel oil, and on top of the base was another can, the size of a tuna fish can. The bottom was off the smaller can, and a small slit was made with a knife at the top. A piece of cloth from an old T-shirt was used as a wick. If you stayed close, the light was adequate. You know the soot that collects on the inside of the chimney of an oil lamp? Well, it collected on the walls. It collected on the ceiling. It collected on everything else. Most of all, it collected on me.

In day-to-day business, I was called Doc John or just Doc. My radio call sign was Charlie Two Squid. In a firefight, if a Marine shouted out Doc, Corpsman, or Medic, the NVA had been trained to look for the next man moving around and to shoot him if they could. We knew a few words of Vietnamese, and they had been taught a few words of English. The three favorite targets for the NVA were our leaders (usually a lieutenant), our communications people (the radioman), and the corpsman (me). The thinking seemed to be if a Marine knew he had no one to treat his wounds, he would be less likely to attack.

Every time the engineers blew up a section of the perimeter, I would take cover in my bunker. With each explosion, the soot would rain down from above, covering my skin and clothing. When I came out of the door, my clothes and skin would be as black as a chimney sweep. When I brushed my clothing, it sent up a little cloud of dust around me. Sergeant Dave Murray, Second Squad Leader, and my friend, witnessed this little scene and broke into uproarious laughter, and thus I was dubbed "Pig Pen," after the character in the Peanuts comic strip written by Charles Schultz. From then on, in Second Platoon Charlie Company if I was needed, you were most likely to hear, "Pig Pen! Get your ass up here."

Through the night, we stood watch behind the circular sandbagged wall. We actually felt fairly secure due to the steepness of the mountainsides. Our only really vulnerable spot was the trail that went out along the saddle over to 1015. I kept my pistol belt hooked around the post that supported one end of the bunk stack so it would be within easy reach if needed. On one occasion, the Marine who was going out to stand his watch decided that rather than carry his M-16, he would borrow my pistol. A round was in the chamber, but the safety was on, which was my usual practice while in the bush. In the darkness of the bunker, he somehow managed to drop the pistol, and as bad luck would have it, the impact was just right to cause it to fire. The noise of the discharge inside our small room awoke the five of us who were sleeping. At first, I just lay very still, taking inventory of all my body parts. Since nothing felt damaged, I quickly reached for my pistol and, to my dismay, grabbed an empty holster.

"Shit! Anybody hit?" I asked.

I realized that the door was still closed so someone turned on a flashlight. While being very concerned that my pistol was missing, I was more worried that somebody had been shot. The light revealed to me four very anxious faces and one rather pale and concerned-looking individual standing in the middle of us. Fortunately for all, the weapon had landed barrel down and discharged into the dirt floor. No one had been injured, with the exception of one man's pride. I did have a few choice words to say with regard to "borrowing" my weapon without permission. He apologized to us all as he took his own rifle and went to stand his watch. I broke the pistol down and cleaned it, making sure the barrel was free of any dirt. Then I went back to sleep with my 45 safely tucked under the sweatshirt that I used for a pillow.

The medical business was, thankfully, very slow, so to keep myself busy I explored every nook and cranny of our compound. One of the luxuries I discovered in a supply bunker was a supply of B-rations. They were stored in cans about the size of three-pound coffee cans. Of course they were olive green in color, and upon reading the labels, oh wow! They contained dehydrated foods such as green beans, carrots, mashed potato flakes, French onion soup, and steaks. Yes! Be still, my beating heart! I had found real beef, and all we needed to do was add water and wait awhile. A couple more men joined me. Then we found a steel shelf rack that would substitute as a grill. We made a big batch of mashed potatoes, the onion soup thick enough to be used as gravy, and with some veggies, we had what was to us the equivalent of a holiday feast. As two of us were busy with food preparation, the word was passed along.

"Everyone is having grilled steaks for supper!"

We all agreed that this meal was a welcome break from C-rations.

Before too long, we received a visit from a general, who arrived in a UH-1 Huey helicopter. New wire was now in place; the fighting positions and bunkers had been reinforced; and the damaged Sea Knight was gone. He was satisfied that Junior and his men could return safely. For us, it was good-bye 950 and off to other places.

## SWEEP AROUND STUD

Maybe we took some incoming mortars or maybe someone sighted enemy movement in the area. Whatever the reason, we received word that the company was going on an extended patrol. For a couple of days, we would sweep the ridge along the east flank of VCB. By Vietnam standards, the weather was cold. It was all the way down to seventy-eight degrees, and the sky was overcast. Monsoon season had arrived. The first day was undulating landscape that was easygoing and without incident. The next day, the rain started. With the cool conditions and lack of any enemy contact, we rapidly reached the top of the ridge and sat overlooking the base. By nightfall, the rain was coming down hard and steady.

That night probably ranks among the top three most miserable nights of my life. I believe that most, if not all, of the guys would share this feeling. The ground was just plain rock. There was nowhere that even closely resembled a level spot. Cold and wet to the bone, we could see the base and our cozy bunkers in the valley below. I picked out a relatively smooth spot on the sloping hill and set up my poncho pup tent. In spite of my best efforts to make a water-diverting dam uphill from my sleeping spot, I still had a small stream of water running between my shoulder blades and around my fanny all night long. For once, I was actually wearing my sweatshirt. I took my shift on radio watch and then tried to catch some sleep. On that cold wet mountain, I spent the night shivering and thinking of home.

The eastern sky finally lightened. We got up and began moving to generate some body heat and work off the stiffness. I would say we awoke, but I'm not sure any of us had actually slept. Our mission had been completed, and we were to be airlifted back down to base. The weather was keeping the Sea Knights on the ground for now, so we sat up there looking at our base and waiting for a break in the weather. We were tired and wet, but willing to wait an hour or so for a ride home.

It was then our new gung ho, everybody-has-one-of-these-guys, company commander. I will call him Captain Hicks. He decided we would not wait for the helicopters. Since we could see the base, we would just walk back to it. For the next seven hours, we crossed some of the worst terrain I had ever been on. With full packs, we were free climbing on slopes that should have been approached with ropes and technical climbing gear. We were climbing straight up and down the jagged rock ridges coming off the main ridge. A couple of hours into our journey, when the sun came out, it felt like we were doing it in a sauna. All of us had wet boots and socks, and the sharp edges of the rocks were taking their toll on our hands and feet.

We had no choice now but to hump the rest of the way out. The helicopters had no place to land, and they had been reassigned to other duties. When we reached the valley floor, my feet were raw and bleeding, as were those of the majority of the troops. We sat along the trail just outside the base's wire, while Captain Hicks jogged up and down the line of bone-tired Marines. He was expounding on how tough we were and how proud of ourselves we should be. At that point, all I felt was trashed and betrayed. We had heard the Sea Knights flying for the past five hours, this could have been done so differently.

For the next few days, I treated a lot of very ugly and damaged feet, including my own, and listened to a lot of complaints about leadership.

## SEA KNIGHTS, HUEYS, AND JOLLY GREEN GIANTS

The rotary-winged aircraft really came into its own during the Vietnam era. I would be remiss not to discuss them. In the early years when our ground troops were limited to mostly advisors, the UH-34 was already seeing service. These aircraft had a body shape that resembled a very large grasshopper with a large horizontal rotor over the raised cockpit and a small vertical rotor on the tail. They had three-wheeled landing gear with two wheels in front and one at the tail. The cargo/troop compartment made up the belly of this bird and must have offered some degree of protection for the pilots. I do not know their lifting strength, but it appeared that they could have fit twelve to fifteen troops in this compartment, although fifteen would have been a really tight fit. The door out of the bay was only large enough for one man at a time to exit, and that would have been a weak spot at a hot LZ. They also had a much slower forward speed in comparison to the newer birds, and armament was minimal. The only ones I observed were in the command of the South Vietnamese forces.

The "Gnat" resembled the bubbled helicopters seen in the TV show M*A*S*H*, only it was smaller. It held a maximum of two men in the cockpit. There was a large rotor over the cockpit, with metal skin along the tail, no tail rotor, but two small wings that stood up in a V shape. It had skids for landing gear. I believe it was actually called a "Loch" for light observation combat helicopter that could be fitted with rocket pods, but was usually unarmed. Speed and rapid mobility were its main defenses. The darn things seemed to be able to turn on a dime and their up-and-down capability was just as awesome. They flew like gnats buzzing around your head. It was in one of these that my friend Rich, an Army pilot, once took a pilot who was newly in country up for an orientation flight. As he tells the story, he found a hole in the jungle canopy and dropped through. It must have looked like the airborne motorcycles shown in the movie *Star Wars*.

*During the process of flying beneath the treetops, I crossed paths with an NVA patrol. They started to fire on my helicopter with AK-47s and RPGs. I dodged tree trunks and bullets while looking for another hole big enough to fly through. I found my escape route, but my white-knuckled passenger was so shaken that I doubted the guy would ever get into another helicopter.*

I think it would be a safe bet the new guy would not ever get into another helicopter with Rich. My friend Rich lived by a simple philosophy:

*I was told that Uncle Sam was providing all the beer and bullets we could use. So I tried to make as many of both of these items mine as I could.*

From the ground looking up, it resembled a large tadpole. The UH-1 "Huey" was a Utility Helicopter, with one large rotor on the roof, a small tail rotor, large side doors, and skids for landing gear. The pilot and copilot sat side by side just in front of the central bay. They carried a four-man crew of two pilots, a crew chief, and a door gunner and announced their arrival with a distinctive *thwump thwump* sound that I could feel in my belly even before hearing it. I can still identify that sound today.

As best as I can recall, they all had M-60 machine guns mounted near the front of each door, where both the crew chief and gunner could fire if need be. The mounting bracket of the M-60 tended to restrict the ability to aim it in certain areas, so most of the door gunners suspended their weapons on bungee cords, which gave them much greater flexibility in aiming. Hueys came in at least two basic configurations. The "Slick" could carry supplies and/or troops, usually six to eight passengers, and was often used in medical evacuations or dust-offs or for mass insertion or pickup of troops. The "Gunship" was fitted with machine guns and two to four rocket pods. While the gunships could have probably carried troops, usually they did not because of the weight of the weapons.

Using as many Slicks as needed to carry the troops, the Army Air Cavalry units would usually ride these into battle. Several gunships escorted them. As the troops went into the LZ, gunships would circle around them, providing any enemy in the area a good reason to keep their heads down.

Army pilots also flew in support of our landings from time to time, escorting dust-offs, and even in support of troops meeting heavy combat on the ground. They could deliver remarkably accurate close support with both their rockets and door guns. Many a "grunt" (infantry solider) is here today because of them. Like the GPV (general purpose vehicle), commonly known as the Jeep of earlier combat days, the Huey was the workhorse of the battlefields of Vietnam. It had good speed and distance capabilities.

Toward the middle of my tour of duty, the Cobra arrived. About the same length and rotor configuration of the Huey, it was strictly an attack gunship with six rocket pods, two to four machineguns mounted on outriggers, and a nose-mounted mini-gun and grenade launcher. The two-man crew, a pilot and weapons officer, sat one behind the other as the helicopter body was much narrower. With a good distance range, excellent air speed, and maneuverability, it could prowl the sky in support of other aircraft or ground troops. The Cobra had a dive speed, when coming in on attack, in excess of 100 miles an hour, making it a very difficult target for the enemy to bring down.

The Sea Knight UH-46 was the heavy hauler for the Navy and Marines. It had two large rotors, one up front near the cockpit, and the second on a raised tailfin at the back. It had tricycle landing gear and side doors just behind the cockpit. These doors usually had the top half removed to accommodate the M-60 machine guns. The back of the floor lowered down to create a ramp for loading and unloading. A section of the floor could also be lifted out to create a belly door. With the same four-man crew type as a Huey, these birds could carry fifteen to seventeen troops and usually had canvas stretched along each side for seating. They could also pick up small artillery guns, jeeps, large nets filled with food, ammo, water, or whatever was needed and deliver it to the troops in the field. They were frequently used in dust-off service. With only an M-60 machine gun mounted in each front door, they depended on gunships for support. They had reasonable speed, excellent range, and they were strong. Sea Knights were my usual in-country mode of transportation.

The Army had the UH-47 "Chinook," which had the same body style as the Sea Knight, only a little bit wider, with a four-point wheeled landing gear, and more weight-carrying capacity. They carried about twenty-five fully armed troops and were painted a deeper shade of brownish green.

The UH-53 "Sea Stallion," also known as the "Jolly Green Giant," was a big helicopter. It was shaped like a Huey but was apparently much better fed as a youngster! It had a rear ramp like the 46 and 47 birds and could carry over thirty troops, large pallets of supplies, and a couple of jeeps. With cables or nets underneath, the UH-53 was able to lift large artillery guns, vehicles, or *Boo Coo* supplies. It also came in another very unusual configuration that we called the flying crane. The entire loading bay was absent and the wheels were mounted on side struts, making it resemble a giant dragonfly. It could pick up a damaged 46 and carry it back for repairs. It could also set down on a modular unit such as a Con X box, half of a semi-truck trailer, clamp onto it, and carry it wherever it was needed. This would be a great way to move a prebuilt surgical unit up closer to the troops.

Even with their many elaborate capabilities, helicopters were still just pieces of machinery. What made them special were the amazing pilots and crews. These courageous young men took us into and out of some very tight spots. I remember one occasion in particular.

A Marine had slipped and fallen in a rocky dry riverbed and had badly injured his back. The sides of the gully were very steep, and since I did not want to move him too much, my plan was to have the helicopter (in this case a Sea Knight) hover above us while we would lift him straight up through the bay door. The pilot settled the belly of his bird down into this gully and held an amazingly steady hover with his front rotor only three to four feet off the ground. The patient was placed onboard as planned and flown out without a hitch. The only change that was made in my plan was to remove me from the area. They wanted me unharmed, just in case this didn't work out and the helicopter crashed. Nice to know I was needed.

Several years later, I would be working at Douglas Community Hospital with a man named Mike Bertalan, who was the hospital's purchasing agent. The two of us were driving back from a seminar we had attended in Lansing, and in our conversation to pass the time, we discovered that we had both been in Vietnam at the same time. He had been a Marine Corps helicopter pilot and flew Sea Knights. Complimenting him and his fellow pilots, I shared the above and several other dust-off stories that had impressed me enough to be able to recall them. It was a good-sized country, and a lot of Americans were spread all over it. I was fairly sure that it was unusual enough just to meet somebody who was there at the same time. Oddly enough, he asked me if I happened to remember the number of the helicopter or the unit insignia. His unit had a silhouette of a cartoon character, "Zeke the Wolf" on the tail fin, and he recalled a similar situation. The emblem sounded familiar, but I honestly could not remember the number. That evening when I was home, I took out some of my old photos and looked through them. Indeed, I had taken a picture of the rescue. Sure enough, with the help of a magnifying glass, the number was visible on the side of the helicopter. It matched that of Mike's bird. The next day, when I laid the picture on his desk, all he could say was, "I don't think I would have done that if I had known my rotors were that close to the ground." I gave him the picture.

As fate would have it, three of my good friends over the years, Bob Acton, Mike Bertalan, and one of my best friends Rich Kiernan, were all former helicopter pilots in Vietnam. I know that in the case of at least two of them, our life paths had crossed many years before we actually met.

## LZ MOON

Sergeant Brookshire was a replacement for one of our guys who had served his tour and rotated back to The World. When he joined us, he was a bit on the plump side for a Marine. One of the first things he did was to hand me his prescription bottle of diet pills.

"Here, Doc, I won't be needing these over here."

He was right, of course; the constant walking and lack of snack foods kept us all very fit and trim, if not a bit underweight. He knew what conditions were like because this was his second tour of duty in country. He was from the tobacco state of North Carolina and enjoyed smoking his pipe. Back in The World, he drove race cars. I enjoyed listening to his tales of the racetrack. It also told me what an adrenaline junkie he was and explained why he was back in this mess a second time.

His arrival occurred as we were once again boarding Sea Knights on our way to a site called LZ Moon. The place sort of looked like a moonscape covered with bomb craters, except that it was very green. The landing was, thankfully, not challenged, and we quickly moved out. NVA troops in the area were not blind or deaf, and it was always to our advantage to be some other place than where they thought we were. As usual, moving out meant going uphill. Our path was fairly steep and our packs fully loaded. Yet another day of sweating in the heat and humidity. The steady uphill climb and the intense sun were taking their toll on me. So I got to thinking I had this bottle of diet pills in my bag, which usually provided an energy boost, so why not take one? In about fifteen minutes, I was walking up the side of the mountain like it was level ground, handing out salt tablets and encouraging the troops to drink plenty of water to prevent heat stroke. This also stopped much of the grumbling and complaining because they were Marines, and if a damn sailor could walk this hill in this heat, they were not about to say they couldn't. Pushing my own body that hard, I became aware that my heart rate was skyrocketing, and I sat down and counted my pulse, which by now was racing at 180 beats per minute. I reached in my pack and dumped the diet pills over the side of the mountain.

Midafternoon came without incident, and we found ourselves in a very pleasant grassy spot along a cool mountain river. Every one of us was feeling the effects of the heat, and it was decided that a good cooling-off would be beneficial for all. So while half the platoon set up a hasty perimeter, the other half went for a swim. To replace the sodium we had all perspired away, I made sure that salt tabs were handed to everyone as the refreshed troops traded places with the security.

There were some wild orange trees growing nearby and the fruit was ripe. So we harvested a few. A wild orange in Indochina starts out about the same size as the kind we are used to, but the skin was six times as thick so the edible fruit was approximately plum-sized and tasted like any other orange. We picked several more and stuffed them in our packs for later. Canteens were filled, and with all the men refreshed, hydrated, and a bit rested, we continued our mission. We humped another click and, later in the day, found a good spot to dig in for the night.

After a quiet night, we were on the move again the next morning. We were walking just inside a taller brush line along a ridge for cover. One fire team of four men was out on the right flank to prevent any surprises, and to our left was a broad grassy field that stretched close to a half mile before it rose to a parallel ridge. As I looked out across the area, something just did not seem right. The opposite ridge was a bit lower than the one we were on and was covered in thigh-high grass just like the field except in one spot, about halfway up the ridge, where a clump of two or three trees, five to seven foot tall, were sticking up. They looked very dry compared to the rest of the lush vegetation. I dropped back to find Lieutenant Webster to point it out and tell him of my suspicions.

"LT, I am pretty sure that is a cave entrance over there," I said, pointing toward the ridge.

He called in my suspicion to the company commander and was told that he could go check it out, but I think he had his doubts. It meant walking nearly a full click out in the open. It was near 100 degrees in the shade, if there had been any shade. We spread out and began our approach cautiously. You could almost hear the thoughts of the men as we moved out.

"This is a f—king wild-goose chase."

"What would a crazy squid know about a cave?"

"This is dry land, and he's a sailor."

"Boy, is this ever a waste of time and sweat!"

We crossed the field without being shot at. When we finally arrived at the site, sure enough, the brush had been placed there to either conceal or mark a tunnel entrance. Since no one was at home and we could not find any trip wires or booby traps, Lieutenant Webster called it in, and we did a bit of looking around while we waited for further orders. As we explored, we found that it was a rather extensive complex, with a kitchen, sleeping quarters, and an operating room complete with a surgery table and cabinet filled with medical gear. It might have been set up as a forward aide station. There were also caches of food, ammunition, and weapons there. When the engineers arrived, they destroyed it as best they could. Chalk one up for "The Squid!"

We continued our sweep of the area over the next couple of days, finding a few more stashes of arms, food, and supplies. At some point, I don't remember just how, I had torn the inseam of my trousers, five to six inches down each leg. I was out of suture material, or I would have sewn the seams closed. I had done a makeshift repair using wire from around a C-ration carton to staple the tear. This was not a wholly (pun intended) satisfactory solution. While it did protect vital and sensitive parts of my anatomy from cuts and scratches from the brush and saw grass, the ends of the wire were sharp and presented their own risks. Walking a bit bowlegged worked most of the time, but moving fast or ducking for cover was a different story, and we did get into a number of minor firefights. I received several minor pokes and scratches on my thighs from my makeshift staples. Remember, I mentioned that it was *not* advisable to wear underwear in the jungle heat and humidity? The constant moisture from rain and sweat increased the potential for developing a fungal infection, commonly called jungle rot, which was bad enough on our feet. My makeshift repair also provided a degree of modesty as well as protection.

## CHIPPENDALES IN VIETNAM?

For some unknown reason, instead of resupplying us in the field and moving us to a new spot, we were flown back to Camp Carroll for food, water, and bullets. It was to be a quick turnaround since we were needed in another location.

At the time, one of the men had an infected abscess on his left cheek near his nose, and it was not responding very well to the treatment I was able to do out in the bush. It really needed to be incised, drained, and kept clean for a few days. There was no way I could do that in the bush, but I now had another option. Camp Carroll was a fairly large base and would have an aide station. After obtaining permission from Lieutenant Webster, we went in search of a doctor. It took a little while, but we did find the Regimental Aide Station (RAS). I explained the situation to one of the station's corpsmen. The doctor checked him over and agreed with my assessment. Surgery and some serious antibiotics were needed; he would remain on the base for treatment and rejoin us in a few days. We hotfooted it back to the staging area near the LZ to pick up his gear. I had replenished my medical supplies at the RAS while the doctor examined him. I still needed to grab some food.

I asked my patient to pick up a new pair of trousers for me before he came back out to us. He pointed out that we were both the about the same size, so why not trade now. That made good sense to me. His were intact, and I would be a lot more comfortable. In the meantime, he would be able to find a supply tent and get two new pairs. We were about to head over to a nearby tent to make the exchange when somebody yelled out.

"Here come the choppers!"

We had no time to waste, and seeing that it was only us guys, we thought what the heck. Standing face to face, about three feet apart, we hastily ripped off our packs and trousers along the side of the road. The sight of our frenzied haste must have been comical. The trade completed, I grabbed some meal boxes from those left over. I would not be getting my favorites, but I wouldn't go hungry. I headed for the helicopter. He went off to RAS to be treated.

About five days later, my patient rejoined us in the field, brought the new trousers, and shared, as Paul Harvey used to say, the rest of the story. After the doctor had lanced and drained his facial abscess, he decided to go over and see the USO show that was being put on that afternoon. At some point during the show, the Master of Ceremony (not Bob Hope) gave a special thanks to the two Marines that had entertained the show company's ladies that morning down at the airport. It seems they had been sitting in a closed jeep not far from our staging area. They must have been quite perplexed, as we stood an arm's length apart frantically tearing off our clothing. Since it was a little late for embarrassment, we all just had a good laugh.

To the ladies wherever you may be today, you're welcome, and congratulations! You got to see my entire Chippendale career.

## PILLAGE AND PLUNDER

Back out in the bush, we continued to search the area for the enemy and/or their supplies. Along the way, we came upon a Montagnard village that, after watching for a while, we determined was empty. We moved in with caution and noticed that it probably had not been abandoned long. Based on the weed growth, the gardens had been well tended up until two or three weeks ago. We surmised that the villagers had most likely been taken by the NVA to be supply bearers. Rumor had it that it was not uncommon for the NVA to use the native people as forced labor.

These Montagnards are native tribal people who live in the mountains of the Indochina (Cambodia, Laos, Thailand, and Vietnam) Peninsula. Very much like our Native American Indians, they loved and respected the land and did not have any use for lines on maps that marked borders. They had no love for the NVA. Many of the young men served as scouts and guides for American and ARVN military units (Army of the Republic of

Vietnam). While the locals tended to treat them as second-class citizens, the US troops had a great deal of respect for these tough resilient people. I would much rather go into a fight with four Montagnards at my side than any platoon of ARVN I met. I felt a special kinship to these people probably due to my own Native American heritage.

The thatched hut houses used by the Montagnard people were called hooches. At one point, a Marine thought he saw movement inside a hooch. He was one of our new reinforcements, an FNG who had just arrived in country. He must have seen way too many John Wayne movies because, in classic war movie style, the FNG ran up to the door, backhanded a grenade in, and flattened his body against the wall between the door and window. As I watched this outstanding act of courage from about fifty feet away, I just shook my head, knowing that in ten seconds or so I would be going to work picking scrap metal out of his butt. Apparently, he got to thinking, but what he failed to consider was that the home was made of bamboo and grass, neither of which does a very good job of slowing down shrapnel. The grenade exploded. By the time he yelled "Medic!" I was already moving rapidly toward him. His helmet, pack, and flak jacket protected him from the waist up, but he had several nonlife-threatening wounds to his arms, legs, and fanny. As I was tying the battle dressings to his wounds, I could not help myself.

"So when they give you a Purple Heart, and they will give you one, are you working on a good story to explain these wounds? Self-inflicted doesn't have a very heroic ring to it."

Someone found a suitable site for a dust-off; with his wounds stabilized, he was headed for the hospital ship. I could not help but inwardly laugh as I projected into the future.

*Tell us why they gave you that Purple Heart Ribbon again, Daddy.*

He spent a couple of weeks recovering from his wounds and eventually rejoined us. I can't say the same for the poor chicken that had been in the hooch. She became our supper.

Along the edge of one of the garden paths, I harvested a dozen or so ripe red peppers. They were no bigger than my thumb, and I tucked them into a foil pouch from C-rations. A very small amount mixed into a can of C-rats spiced up the flavor of the meals, which by this time had become kind of boring. Just those few peppers lasted me for a couple of months even with sharing. They were very hot so a little went a long way.

We had discovered a few NVA supplies in the village and placed them all inside one of the hooches, which we planned to burn as we left. At that time, we had no engineers with us. We left ammunition rounds in the chambers of the rifles so that when they heated up or cooked off, it would make the weapons unusable. As we started to pull back from the area, I was joking with Sergeant Brookshire and mentioned that I was now over six months in the bush and had not once gotten to pillage or plunder. Since it was very unlikely that the residents of the village would be returning, I requested permission to burn the hooch. When the platoon had gone a safe distance, we each lit a sterno tablet. We all carried these as a heat source for warming our meals. We threw them into the building and took off running. As we jumped into a ravine, forty yards down the trail, the hooch blew sky-high. There were multiple secondary explosions. Apparently, a much larger store of ammo that we had not discovered had been hidden under the floor.

"You probably should not let me do that again," I said to Sergeant B.

## WHEN PIG PEN FLIES

The next couple of days were uneventful, always a good thing in my line of work. It was back on the helicopters for a forward hop to try and catch up to, or get ahead of, a retreating enemy. I was first in line at the drop ramp on the left side of the bird, with Lieutenant Webster directly across from me on the right. The pilot passed word back that our gunship escorts were reporting enemy movement in the area, so we could expect a "Hot LZ." This meant we were very likely to be offloading while being shot at. So I got to thinking that the shooting would start when the ramp got to the full down position, and I had no intention of being in that doorway when the bullets started flying. The ramp started down as we descended. We were the first chopper in with the number two bird right behind. Two more Sea Knights were about a quarter mile behind us, with two Huey gunships circling above them. The ramp was level with the deck in the half-way-down position, and the ground looked to be about eight feet below us. Pushing off using the inside rail to give me some speed, I ran out of the back of the Sea Knight. I sort of remember that Lieutenant Webster's arm came reaching out to grab me, but it was too late. I was gone. My plan was to hit the ground running and be in an empty bomb crater about twenty yards away before the shooting even started. I remember thinking, as I continued to fall through the air, that I should be on the ground by now. I went very loose in the knees and hips, and when I finally did hit land, I rolled to my right. At this point, I was on my back, looking up at the Sea Knight that was still some twenty feet in the air, still above the elephant grass, and still descending. Rolling to my feet and drawing my weapon, I scampered to the crater. Having just left an aircraft that was somewhere above the roof line of an average two-story house, with a fully loaded pack on my back and having not broken my fool neck or a couple of legs, was a minor miracle. Now I had another *big problem*. No Marine helicopters on the ground meant no Marines on the ground. Now the circling gunships had definite movement in a suspected Hot LZ. Very soon, I was watching dust puffs in the dirt as M-60 rounds from the gun bird's door gunner were impacting in a nice straight line headed directly at me. If I was going to die here, I was at least going to go defiantly. I rolled over on my back and saluted them with a very common American hand gesture involving my middle finger. The message was received, and the bullets stopped about five feet away. As it turned out, the LZ was quiet after all, so after all four helicopters had landed, Lieutenant Webster checked the map, made a plan, and we moved out on foot.

We did not make any direct contact but received daily harassment from mortars. That told us we were pushing the NVA unit hard. None of the platoon had been fatally wounded; only a handful were sent out with shrapnel wounds before our air cover finally located and neutralized our problem. With the enemy no longer in the area, we were once again pulled back for a couple of days' rest on the defense lines, but this time they took us to Rock Pile.

## THE ROCK PILE

Located between Camp Carroll and VCB, on a very large flat-topped butte along Highway 9, Rock Pile was an artillery base that provided support for much of the surrounding area. The guns stationed here were some our largest, and with the help of someone on the down-range end in radio contact, they could lob shells several miles away very accurately. It was quiet when we arrived and took our positions, relieving the troops that had been on lines. I dropped my pack and walked the line so that I would know where the troops were located. This was something that I would do every time we sat in. There were times when we would be attacked at night, and I needed to memorize the area so that I had an idea of the safest route to take to anywhere they were dug in. With this task completed, I sat down with three other men, heated some C-rations for supper, and began eating, unaware that I was right in front of one of the guns. The brush was so thick between the gun emplacement and me that there had been no reason to check that direction. Apparently, somebody needed a fire mission right then because, all of a sudden, there was a very large *Kaboom* directly behind me. My supper went flying, and by the time I heard the *M* in *Kaboom*, I was lying on my belly, my 45 out and cocked with the safety off. I was ready to return fire; my brain quickly started putting the pieces together, and I realized what had happened. We were all a little stunned by both the noise and my reaction to it, but later it gave us a good laugh.

By now, I was carrying my 45 in a quick-draw shoulder holster that had been given to me by some of the men. They did not tell me if they had bought it or just borrowed it for the war. I didn't ask. On hot, dry days, it hung outside my flak jacket away from the sweat as I perspired. On rainy days, I slipped it through the armhole to be carried inside the jacket out of the rain. I sweated less when it rained. It could be out and ready very quickly from either location.

You might think that sleeping would be next to impossible in this situation, but while the smallest abnormal sound of potential danger would wake us up, the knowledge that this was not a threat, the relative safety of our location, and fatigue, all combined to make sleep not only possible but restful. We only spent about three days online at Rock Pile and were once again taken back to VCB to load up our packs. According to the rumor mill, we were going back up to Khe Sanh.

# KHE SANH REVISITED

This company-sized operation was to contact an observed enemy presence in the area. The plan was to find, engage, and destroy enemy forces. You could always tell when somebody had been in the Khe Sanh area because his boots, clothing, and equipment would be the color of red clay. This was the only area that I remember where there was so much clay; I could not help but think this would be a great place to open a pottery business. When the ground was dry, it had the consistency of concrete covered with a quarter inch of fine red dust that settled on everything. It was darned near impossible to dig a cat hole to relieve yourself, let alone make a good fighting hole. That was not the worst of it though; when the ground became wet, and it rained daily when we were in Monsoon season, the clay mud stuck tenaciously to everything. After fifteen minutes of walking, we were all an inch or two taller and carrying an extra three to five pounds of mud on each boot, making walking that much harder. The stuff was very slimy and slippery. It was like trying to walk on ice. Every time we slowed down or stopped, using the edge of a rock or a stick, we tried to scrape as much off as we could. Trying to dig in the wet variety of this stuff was equally as difficult as digging the dry clay. Only now it would cling to your entrenching tool and whatever you used to try and scrape it off. It brought to mind a comedy skit of Laurel and Hardy, trying to pull flypaper off one hand only to have it stick to the pulling hand.

One of the things I may not have mentioned about the unit was their ability to move quickly and quietly, which made it possible to surprise the NVA. The sun was out, making it hot and humid. We were moving along a wooded ridge when the point man signaled a halt. We had been moving along so silently that the woodland creatures along the way, either did not hear us or by the time they did, it was safer for them to hunker down and not move. I was about the seventh man in the line of march, and when we stopped, a deer that was about six feet from me became nervous, bolted from its cover, and ran down the hillside. Even though it scared the dickens out of me, had we not been moving in on some NVA troops, we would most likely have had venison for supper that night. My 45 was drawn, with the safety off, while he was still very much in range.

The NVA were dug in well and had a fairly strong position on a hill when we found them. Captain Hicks was determined to take them on, and his basic plan was to hit them hard right up the middle, counting on the ferocity of the young men in his command to bring success. A lesson from my tenth grade US History teacher, Ms. Agustie, kept running through my mind:

"Never do a frontal assault on a fortified position. You will suffer a greater number of casualties by doing so," she had said.

The battle on that morning was fierce and intense, but due to the alertness of the platoon and squad leaders, we had few casualties. In the fluidness of the battle, they very effectively used fire concentrations and a double flanking maneuver to secure the hill.

After extracting our wounded, we continued to pursue the remainder of the enemy force. Because we had used a lot of ammo in our attack, we called for a resupply and moved out again. The second platoon was to sweep around the base of the hill, where the rest of the company was positioned. Since the sides of this particular hillside were quite steep, and the waist to chest-high brush was very thick, we picked our way cautiously and silently along the rocky bottom of a small creek bed. The only sound was the soft movement of the wind through the leaves and the gentle gurgle of a foot-wide rivulet bouncing merrily over and around the stones as it flowed toward the valley below. Even with the constant knot of fear in my stomach and the fact that all the senses had been honed to razor sharpness, it was the kind of place that could make me forget for just a few moments that there was a war going on around us. We eventually reached our objective, just a spot on the map, and set in for the night.

While the day had been cloudless and beautiful, during the night the monsoon rains moved back in. There was now a steady shower falling on our night ambush/listening post half a click out. It was a long, uneventful night that changed from black to dark gray, the day creeping in on heavy clouds that prevented any real sunrise.

Our original plan was to sweep back to the company position around the base of the hill and come up the opposite side from where we had come down the day before. But the clay was so slippery, and the brush so thick, that we changed the plan and went back to the creek bed. The previous day, the water had been a foot wide and an inch deep with four to five feet of dry rocks and sand on either side. Today was different. The water was three feet wide, and the wet rocks offered much less secure footing. Soon, the bottom of the wash was full of reddish brown water that reached our knees. We were moving along at a good speed since we wanted to use this brush-free path as long as we could. By the time we arrived at the previous entry point, yesterday's quiet little stream was chest deep and six to eight yards wide. Weapons were held high as we navigated the treacherous water.

Finally, we left the river to start back up the trail and join the main body of our company. After two hours of three steps forward, then sliding one step back on the slick red clay of the hillside, we arrived back at our perimeter. We were soaking wet and bone-tired. I cleaned and dried my pistol, made a brief health check round of the men, and went back to our platoon command post. I reported the overall condition of the troops to Lieutenant Webster and Sergeants Christiansen and Brookshire while heating a can of C-rats. It was still raining as I tied the corners of my poncho up to create a night shelter, a futile gesture since everything was already as wet as it could get. As night descended around us, I lay down and tried to get some sleep before it was my turn to take watch.

As I lay there that night, still soaked, cold to the bone, and unable to drift off to sleep, I thought about my father. It was December 22, his birthday. It somehow seemed significant that on this day, I, a twenty-one-year old, was wearing my country's uniform, trying my best to do a good job in the jungles of Vietnam. How ironic it was that during World War II, my father, a twenty-one-year old, was wearing his country's uniform, trying his best to do a good job on a US Navy Destroyer in the Pacific Ocean, just to my east.

The rain kept things quiet. A Christmas ceasefire had been issued, so our mission was basically over. The next day, the rain continued and prevented our extraction. In the midafternoon hours of Christmas Eve, the rain stopped and the sky cleared, allowing the Sea Knights to come after us. We packed our wet gear and waited for the thumping sounds of the rotors and our ride home. We usually loaded about fifteen men on a helicopter. We were a long way out, and they did not have a lot of time before dark, so we decided to go with seventeen-man groups. We were very high up in the mountains, and the air was a bit thinner, causing some lift problems for the helicopters. I was on one of the first pair of Sea Knights out, and as we lifted off, what should have been blue sky or maybe the tops of trees out of the window was serious vegetation. The helicopter lurched against the tree limbs, the odor of JP-4 aviation gas becoming very strong, as the pilot dumped half his fuel tank to lighten the aircraft. We then lifted quickly above the trees, and the rest of the men left in fifteen-man groups. We all arrived safely back at VCB, out of the bush for Christmas.

## AN OLIVE GREEN CHRISTMAS

When we arrived back at base, we learned that a shower tent with pumped and heated water had been built down by the river. A hot shower sounded so good to us that a dozen others and I had to go try it out. A poured concrete slab for a floor, with tent sides and no roof, it was great. Multiple showerheads lined the outside edges, and the water, which cascaded out, was hot and strong. As we entered the shower, there were several empty or partially full fifty-five gallon drums into which we dropped our filthy clothing. I'm sure it was classified hazardous waste. We then proceeded to grab a bar of soap and washcloth from a nearby table and take the first real shower many of us had had in several months. After getting clean and dry, there were fresh uniforms stacked up for the taking at the exit. Being clean and in clean clothing was wonderful, and we made our way back up to the company area and a big mail call. Due to the fact that we had been moving around so quickly on this last mission and because there were a lot of Christmas care packages from home, they had held our mail until we could catch up with it. It had already become dark by the time most of us settled down to read our mail and open the packages, but that did not dampen our spirits at all. Mail call and packages from home have always been a high point of every military man's day. The letters helped to keep us focused on why we were doing our best to survive. The care packages I received had all sorts of wonderful items like pictures of my little brother Jack with Judge, the current family dog. I could almost smell the fall foliage of the big maple tree in my parents' front yard. There were newspaper clippings of my brother Jim playing football and wrestling on the high school teams and a photo of Dad standing beside a deer he had harvested with his bow and arrows. There never seemed to be enough pictures of my Mom or girlfriend. There were audiotapes/letters with the voices from home and the current music, books to read, instant soups, and Kool-Aid, which helped to improve the taste of water treated with iodine tablets. Then there was Jiffy Pop; I was the platoon champ at cooking Jiffy Pop over a C-4 fire, without burning the popcorn. C-4 was a plastic explosive that came in bars, one inch thick, two inches wide, and ten inches long. Stick a blasting cap and fuse inside, and it created an exploding device, but cut it into thin wafers and light it with a match, and all it did was burn very hot and very fast. It was the GI's field version of microwave cooking.

There were homemade treats to share, like cookies, which sometimes had been so bounced around that we ate them with a spoon. There are few things in life as good as a box of homemade chocolate chip cookie crumbs. Mom had sent a couple of banana nut breads. Some of the men had bought a few cases of beer, and one of the newer guys had even received some good stateside whiskey. His folks ran a liquor store back in the United States and had figured out a way to get it past the post office restriction against mailing liquor; it arrived in eight-ounce plastic baby bottles. When empty, the bottles made great lightweight and waterproof containers to carry my bulk pills. I was able to carry extra salt tablets and malaria pills and still reduce the weight of my pack.

I pulled out a loaf of the banana nut bread and passed it around; we all agreed it was mighty fine eating. The punch line to this story is that there was a small piece left over and later, as I looked at it in the light of day, I would discover several patches of different kinds of molds growing on it. I never told any of the guys, and no one became ill. Penicillin is a bread mold, right?

That night, I crawled under my poncho with a full stomach and a warm buzz from the alcohol. Since another company was assigned to the defensive perimeter, I was able to sleep soundly. Christmas morning, I was awakened early by an unusual sound overhead. I rolled out from under my poncho and looked up at the sky. Above me were two helicopters that looked sort of like Hueys but their bodies were much slimmer. Thinking that the whiskey and beer mix from the night before had damaged my eyesight, I asked a nearby Marine if he noticed anything wrong about those Hueys. He told me that they were the new Cobra helicopters. I was very relieved that my vision was still intact. I joined a couple of others and walked over to a place where we could see the LZ. We watched as the Cobras came in for a landing. Years later, my friend Rich and I, while reminiscing about Vietnam and comparing dates and memories, would discover that he had been the pilot of one of those Cobras. They had dropped in for fuel and breakfast while patrolling our sector on Christmas Day.

## MY CHRISTMAS MIRACLE

There was a point on the Khe Sanh mission when I became aware that my Episcopal Serviceman's Cross, given to me by Harriet's father, was missing from around my neck. It was a silver-colored medallion the size of a half dollar, and I had no idea where or when it had fallen off. I felt very bad for having lost it. Now, I had quite a few miles of jungle behind me after discovering it was missing, I was sitting back at VCB, prying a couple of inches of red clay off the soles of my boots with my K-Bar. Clay was coming off in layers, and as one particularly good-sized chunk came off, my eye caught a glimpse of tarnished metallic color. Embedded in the tenacious red clay was my medallion. I was grateful and relieved that fate had somehow destined I should not lose my keepsake.

# BULLETS WERE NOT THE ONLY DANGERS

You have already read about lightning bolts, snakes, falls, and almost becoming a tiger's breakfast. There were also vehicle accidents, fights, dumb accidents, and the various illnesses that go hand in hand with a large group of people living together anywhere. The relationship between a corpsman and the Marines he lives with and cares for is very special and quite unique. My main responsibility was for their physical health. I cleaned minor cuts, scratches, and abrasions and applied antibiotic and Band-Aids or dressings with the same care I gave to treating battle wounds. I had pills for various symptoms and prevention of malaria. These were all things that made them see me as their "family doctor." Caring for their emotional well-being in this very stressful environment often placed me in the role of confidant, counselor, friend, brother, or, at times, even parent. This was usually a tougher task since I was, quite often, just as stressed and frightened as the man I was trying to help. I learned very well and very quickly to handle my own feelings. In this role, I often found myself dispensing some very unusual "words of wisdom" such as the following:

"When you go on R&R in most of the nearby countries, the hookers are required to have a monthly health check and are licensed. If you decide to seek the services of a hooker, unless you want to bring home an exotic venereal disease as a war souvenir, make sure you ask to see her license."

Sure enough, every so often, someone would return from Hong Kong, Tokyo, Singapore, or any one of several other destinations, take me aside and, in a whispered and embarrassed voice, say, "Doc, I think I got the clap."

"Did you check her papers like I told you to?"

"Well, yes, except for this one who looked so sweet."

Diagnosis was so easy that I could do it from three feet away, and usually did; treatment, however, was much more up close and personal. It required a stroll over to the refrigerator at BAS where we found 1.2 million units of Bicillin for each hip: an injection of about a teaspoon of stuff that looked like and was as thick as Elmer's Glue. So for a few minutes of what I can only hope for his sake was really good sex, he now got to spend the next three days limping on both hips, and it hurt every time he went to the bathroom for a week. Are we having fun yet?

## THAT WAS THE WEEK THAT WAS

Using rocks and bushes for cover, when I could find cover, I had indeed done my share of scurrying around in firefights to get to wounded Marines. Just as important, though, were the daily or routine tasks, which were really made clear to me during the week that I call "The Great Malaria Epidemic." It would once again become apparent to me that I had not cornered the market on letting thinking get in the way of good sense. As mentioned earlier, for the prevention of malaria, we took a small white pill every day, and on every Sunday, a big orange pill. Unknown to me, several of the newer troops decided that being sick in the hospital with clean sheets and a good-looking, round-eyed nurse was preferable to humping through the jungle and being shot at. Every day, I would hand each man his pill(s). As I had moved on, they would toss the tablets out in front of their bunkers or foxholes. If they had been seeds, there would have been a quite a good-sized orchard of pill trees in front of our lines.

As you can guess, it was not too long before somebody was shaking with the chills and running a temperature of 105. So you-know-who was making a bunker call. Like a house call, except the house was a hole in the ground. With no lab work, there was no way to be certain, but even though I knew they had gotten their protection daily, my working diagnosis was malaria. I informed Lieutenant Webster, the sergeants, and the man's squad leader and then took him over to BAS. Dr. Pasker agreed with my initial diagnosis, and the man was flown out to the hospital ship, where lab tests confirmed our suspicions.

For the next seven days, this scene replayed itself again and again. On the fifth day and the fifth patient, I was told, "You got to be kidding, Doc. We can't take any more men off the line and still be able to cover our area."

"All right, troop, go back to your hole and pick up your gear. You're spending the night here with the command post."

"What are you doing, Doc?" Sergeant Christiansen asked.

"You can watch him have a seizure and die. I have a responsibility for the rest of the platoon tonight," I replied.

"Okay, take him to BAS and try not to find any more."

A letter arrived from Harriet during this week. While I was reading it, my friend Gene asked me if there was anything interesting in the letter. Well, she is sad this week. It seems that Shorty, her pet hamster, died. I didn't even know she had a hamster.

By now, I began to suspect that the problem might be something more than new guys who had not had time for the medication to become effective. By checking around and asking questions, it did not take too long to figure out what was going on. I began to reinforce with all the troops the importance of taking their pills. Malaria could kill you right now, and even if you did survive, it would stay in your system for the rest of your life and flare up, over and over, years later. To be very honest, I do not think my words changed very many minds. That happened when the first of my patients returned from the ship. They shared the experience of icy cold showers and baths to bring down the fever, aching all over, and hours of shaking with the chills. This was a far cry from their visions of lying comfortably in clean white sheets on a soft bed and having a beautiful young Lieutenant JG in her crisp white Navy uniform pampering them. Theirs were the words that convinced everyone to start taking their pills again, and that was fine with me as long as it worked. I thought about titling this chapter, "Just Say Yes to My Drugs."

## DON'T DRINK THE WATER

To keep us light and fast, every third to fifth day, food and water were brought to us in the field. We were often advised against drinking water from streams and rivers because it might be poisoned. I had a hard time figuring out just how anyone was going to poison a fast moving stream or why they would contaminate their own source of drinking water. Most of the time, like everyone else, I followed the rules and only used the "safely treated water" that was sent out to us.

We sat in late one night. After receiving food and water, I did my usual recon of the area, locating the position of each fighting hole. Still carrying all my gear, I started making my way toward our platoon command post when I heard an urgent voice call out my name. I dropped my backpack at the side of the trail, keeping my medical gear, and rushed toward the call to find a Marine thrashing on the ground in the middle of a full-blown grand mal seizure. With a flashlight held in my teeth and two or three ponchos draped on top of us to conceal the light, I got an oral airway inserted. With the help of two others, we held him down until the seizure quieted. His skin felt unusually hot, his temperature 104.4 degrees. Before I was able to do anything else for him, a second man began to convulse. A quick wipe of the plastic airway on the leg of my trousers, and I had established an airway on the second man. I assigned a couple of Marines to hold on to him and keep him from injuring himself. I resumed treatment of patient 1, who was now awake and able to take oral fluids and Aspirin, to bring down his fever. I was also keeping an eye on patient 2, who fortunately was only four feet away and also had a fever near 104 degrees. As soon as he was able to take something by mouth, he got his aspirin.

"What is it, Doc?" someone asked me.

"Could be malaria," I replied. "They both have elevated temperatures, but with the nausea and diarrhea, it is most likely a gastrointestinal thing."

It was a bit hectic. Because of the darkness, I was still working under ponchos with a small flashlight held between my teeth. Before long, both Marines were stable, their fevers were down, and they were taking their fluids well.

It was about now that I became acutely aware that my own belly was cramping. *Big time.* I gave my patients' buddies some Aspirin tablets and instructions to follow until I could get back and went to relieve myself. In retrospect, I was probably running a fever myself because my brain was not working very clearly to come up with my next decision. I dropped my medical pack on the trail with my other gear, went up to one of our foxholes, told the Marines not to shoot me, and then walked about fifteen yards in front of our lines in the dark. I dropped my belt and trousers, held onto a tree, and had an explosive episode of diarrhea all over the jungle. That particular foxhole had an extra surprise for any enemy trying to sneak up on them that night. I only half remember weakly crawling back to our lines, finding my pack in the middle of the trail and the soft splat of raindrops falling against my face as I passed out cold over my gear.

I awakened the next morning under the Platoon CP shelter. It seems that when I didn't show up the night before, somebody was sent out to find me. With absolutely no light, I imagine the discovery was made by tripping over me in the dark. Once found, I was dragged out of the rain and back to shelter. The cooling rain most likely prevented me from having a seizure too. The corpsman assigned to the company command group, the Senior Squid, came down to treat me. Unable to give me oral fluids, he had to start an IV line. All through the night, while on their watch, the lieutenant, sergeants and RTOs had taken care of me. Awakening in the morning, I looked around. I was lying with my head turned toward an uprooted tree whose root ball must have been five feet tall. Hanging on a gnarled and broken root stub was a bottle of IV fluid. My eyes followed the tubing down to the spot where it attached to my right arm. They explained what had happened and how Senior Squid had given instructions on how to watch over my IV and what symptoms to be on the lookout for. He had been back to check on both my patients and me.

Right now my bladder was full, and I wanted to go check on my patients. I discontinued the IV line and, on relatively wobbly legs, went to see them. I was very thankful for Senior Squid and his help, but these were my buddies, and their care was my job. While this was probably a bit cornball, and maybe even dumb on my part, it was the way I thought of these men. They were my brothers-in-arms, who would have done and did do the same for me. Their friends were following the instructions given to them by Senior Squid and myself and, although still very weak, they were better. I realized that I did not have my 45 or K-Bar at my side, and thinking back through the events of the previous night, I suddenly remembered that I had left them lying on the ground in front of our lines. Luckily, they were still there when I went to retrieve them. With my fighting gear found, I returned to my patients. Finding that they were still stable, my next thought was how to get them out of the bush. It turns out we had a mail and supply bird on the way. We were able to get them up to the LZ and on their way out.

On my return to Platoon CP, the lieutenant and sergeants appeared to be puzzled as to what I was still doing on the hill. While I did my best to talk them out of it, they sent me back to the LZ with orders to get my "sorry fanny" on a helicopter and get myself treated. I do not think they wanted to spend another night being my nursemaids. On the way back up the trail, I met Captain Hicks. He was coming back from the LZ.

"Good morning, Sir."

"Where are you headed, Doc?"

"Back to the rear to get treatment, Sir."

"Who will take care of your men?"

"With all due respect, Sir, I'm not much good to them in my present condition."

"Doc, if you get on that helicopter, I will see to it that you never get back to this platoon again."

Those were fighting words. The bond I had with my troops was like that of family. Had he not been my senior officer, and had I not been barely able to carry my gear and stay upright, I would have punched him with his smug grin, right then and there. As it turns out, I believe my response was, "F—king fine!"

That may or may not have been followed by "Sir." I still had a fever of over 100 degrees and felt like crap, but I was not about to lose my platoon, and the captain's orders overrode the lieutenant's. I turned and headed back down the path, even more plucked by the fact that we had sent men out on the last bird for R&R. I just hoped we would not get into a firefight any time today since my capacity to work was severely diminished. The captain caught up to me, which was easy at my speed, and placed his hand on my shoulder. It was his way of trying to make me feel better. He told me we were going to stay where we were today. I would be able to rest and see how I felt tomorrow.

About four hours later, word was passed to saddle up. We were moving out. I walked myself up to Company CP and went straight to Captain Hicks and asked to be evacuated. He basically said that we were just going down off the mountain. It was a very short move and would be all downhill. Saying something to the effect that I guessed, if necessary, I could fall downhill, I turned on my heels and rejoined my guys. I may have been a sailor, but I had studied history and been with the Marines long enough to know that you do not defend the low ground. So about midafternoon, down we went. Sure enough, when we reached the bottom, Captain Hicks reached the amazing conclusion that this was a poor spot to defend, and even though it was raining and would be dark in another hour, we would have to go up the mountain in front of us. In the words of Gomer Pyle, "Surprise, surprise, surprise!"

The plan was for the Second Platoon to take the left flank, the Third Platoon the right flank, and the Command Group with the First Platoon to go up the center rather than in one long line. It started to rain again, and I was back on autopilot. I just kept climbing, hand over hand, using tree roots, branches, and rocks to crawl up the steep, wet, slippery mountainside in the dark. We had no idea if the NVA were dug in above us. Just in case the enemy had not yet discovered we were in the area, Captain Hicks had called for artillery flares to be fired overhead, and while they did provide some light to climb, they were also like a big neon sign that said, "Hey, everybody, there are American troops over here."

Our light show was visible for miles in all directions. When the others would stop for a break, I just kept moving, knowing that once I stopped, I wouldn't be able to move again. By the time we reached the top, I was almost on point. As the ground flattened out at the summit, a new "Willy Pete" (white phosphorus) flare popped off almost directly overhead and began a slow descent beneath its parachute. Looking to my left, I saw a Marine down on his hands and knees vomiting. At the same time, the captain approached from my right.

"Glad to see you made it to the top, Doc," he said.

I snapped to attention, explained to him that I had made it by channeling my intense anger for him. I will delete the exact verbs, adverbs, and adjectives actually used in my reply. Now, if he would excuse me, I had a sick Marine who needed my immediate help. I snapped off my very best military salute. The mountaintop was ours without a fight, but fatigue and dysentery had taken their toll. We were pulled out the next morning. It had all been for nothing and, as I would discover later, our amebic dysentery came from one can of untreated water sent out to us by our friends in the rear.

## MORE THAN ONE WAY TO SAVE A LIFE

Back at VCB, the battalion surgeon called me over to his office and asked what had been going on out in the bush. It was a long meeting. I explained to him my handling of the dysentery cases and my frustration concerning my own illness. I also shared with him my concerns with regard to our new company commander. Our casualty rates were going up and morale among the troops was running low, which was uncommon for an elite group like ours. I included, as well as I could, specific situations such as the foot-mangling hike back to VCB and the online assault orders. I really felt that the man, by his actions, was taking unnecessary chances with the lives of the troops under his command and that, while he might go home with a chest full of combat ribbons, it would be at a very high cost of American lives. I did not mind doing my job, and I had a great deal of respect for military discipline, but I had been around long enough to know good tactics from poor ones. I also explained to him that I was not the only one who felt this way. There was a strong possibility that Captain Hicks could become a casualty in the next firefight we were in and that the enemy would probably not be responsible. I told him I would consider his removal good preventative medicine. I was not averse to doing it myself, even though I knew that I wouldn't have to.

As I returned to the platoon area, I could not help but think that Captain Hicks had reported me to the battalion commander, who in turn told the battalion surgeon to talk to me. It was certainly a possibility that disciplinary action, a court-martial and/or time in LBJ (Long Binh Jail our in-country federal prison) for my insubordination, was in my future. I knew the risk of speaking openly, but I also knew that the Marines I was responsible for were taking risks every single day, and they did not deserve to be put in harm's way unnecessarily. It would be my guess that the battalion surgeon talked to the battalion commander and that my case was strong enough and/or my reputation good enough to keep me out of trouble. Within three or four days, Captain Hicks was promoted to commanding a supply company. The action probably saved the life of the captain and a lot of good Marines.

## ADAPTING TO THE ENVIRONMENT

It was sometime along about November or December that I remembered what I had heard when I first joined the company. The usual rotation for a corpsman is to pull the first six months in the bush and the last six in a more secure base. With new people rotating in on a regular basis, everyone was being pulled back after just four months. I was now well into my fifth month and still in the bush with no replacement in sight. The fact was the enemy had become better at shooting corpsmen. Every time a possible replacement came in country, he was pulled to fill in an empty spot in one of the other companies.

A firefight, mortar attack, or ambush was usually ten to fifteen minutes of heart-pounding, adrenaline-pumping, and frantic activity, and then it could be several hours of waiting until it happened again. It is not like what you see in the movies. These seemingly endless minutes and hours were the time when your mind thought of all the worst things it could. To deal with the constant worries and fears of imminent danger, I would keep my mind busy by inventing number systems. We worked with a number system based on ten. In my head, I developed rules for addition, subtraction, multiplication, and division based on every thing from two to twenty place systems. It worked fairly well to push the fear off to the side for a time, but I remained acutely aware of my situation.

The high heat and humidity did not help to make the long periods of waiting around for battles pass any faster. People under stress need some kind of activity to stay sharp. Many of us would carry a paperback book in our pack, and there was always letter writing. A frequent pastime was a card game known as Back Alley Bridge. Played with both jokers in the deck, it involved two to four people. We had the cutthroat, every-man-for-himself, and the partner versions. A full game consisted of twenty-five hands, the first hand being thirteen cards each, the second twelve cards, etc. down to one, and then back to thirteen. The trump suit and bids were made. Points were given on being able to make the bid. A frequently interrupted game could last many days, so one of the players would carry the current score card until the game could be resumed. During a card game was about the only time in the bush you would find four people sitting in a group. The stakes usually were first dibs; the next time, we received C-rations.

Another of my ways to pass the time was to think of plans to end the fighting. One of my thoughts was to build a boxing ring in the DMZ and have President Nixon go ten rounds with Ho Chi Minh, where the winner takes all and the loser goes home. I think Nixon could have taken him. A more ambitious plan involved the CBees bulldozing the country flat, paving the whole thing, painting the appropriate lines, and turning it into a giant parking lot for the Japanese automakers. They could park the cars there until they could load them on ships bound for America. I am sure that idea came to me on a day when I was tired of climbing up and down some mountain.

I was beginning to become a little weary of my overall situation. I still had no dog tags, so obviously, getting killed was against the military rules. I was also sure that the NVA did not know this. I was still in the bush and would probably stay there for the rest of my life. I was considering which arm or leg to stick out of the foxhole during a firefight but always found a reason not to. For example, I need both hands to play the guitar, and I had really become fond of both my feet. I was also acutely aware that I was becoming uncivilized, not the antisocial kind of uncivilized, but the animal instinctual, how-do-I-survive-this-situation uncivilized. Although as a corpsman/medic I was expected and trained to be very observant, I now found that all my senses had kicked into higher gear and I was as skittish as almost every other wild animal in the forest. I knew intimately about hunger, thirst, and potential danger. A broken twig, too green a leaf on the ground, the damp side of a stone facing up when the others around it were dry, and many other things signaled *Be cautious*. I like to think that a part of this was my Indian heritage, and I am sure that the outdoor and hunting lessons taught to me by my father and grandfather helped to keep me alive.

On the subject of seeing stuff along the trail that would indicate the presence of opposing forces, I need to tell you how we handled trash. I am sure the NVA did these things too. Cans and wrappers from food and supplies were buried before breaking camp and the holes brushed over. I would toss a few stones and twigs on the spot so that it looked untouched. GIs smoked a lot, so cigarette butts lying along the trail could be very helpful to the enemy. They could estimate how long ago we were there and how many of us were there. To that end, we would "fieldstrip" the butts as we walked. The paper was torn off in small pieces and rolled between the thumb and forefinger. The resulting scrap was the size of a grain of rice, which if dropped on the trail was soon obliterated by the boot treads of others. The filter material was stripped off in threads and, when teased out, would float like a dandelion seed in the wind and soon be lost in the dense jungle foliage, many yards off the trail. On a windless day, the fine strands could be handled the same way the paper was, and when flipped, they were heavy enough to travel ten feet or more off the trail. The chances of finding a piece of litter so small in the tall grass were slim.

# THON XA VILLAGE

Another interesting operation, which happened shortly after Christmas time, started out with a rapid overnight move. We humped several clicks through the dark of night and by sunrise had completely surrounded the small village of Thon Xa. Our job was to make certain no one left the area while the ARVN searched the village for arms, supplies, ammunition, VC, or NVA sympathizers. This was basically a very cushy assignment. The worst we faced over the next three days was two small boys and a very surly water buffalo. The kids were taking the buffalo out to his usual watering hole and were somewhat surprised to find their way blocked. My guess is that they were not much of a threat, but orders were nobody or nothing was to leave through our lines, so we waved them back. The youngsters got the message that they were not going very far that day, but the buffalo did not. We did not want to shoot him since he was very valuable as a work animal. So after a good deal of prodding by the boys and a couple of shots fired in the air by us, they finally got him turned around and headed back home.

This was farm country, and we were in the midst of rice paddies, fields of grain and vegetables, and orchards of fruit trees. There was another small village less than a click away that had a very interesting cemetery. The graves were mounded aboveground about two feet, which I discovered was because the Vietnamese people were buried in a sitting position. This cemetery was on the grounds of a very beautiful and quaint brick church about the size of a one-room school. It was tall with stained glass windows, such a contrast to the tiny bamboo houses around it. I later learned it was a Catholic church built during the French occupation.

I was going out on at least two patrols a day and soon became very familiar with the area. We had received several replacements, FNGs, during this time, and I often found myself the most senior man on the patrol. The new troops' lack of experience tended to make me more than a bit nervous, so I got to thinking that not one of these guys knew the area as well as I did, and I felt confident enough about the safety in the area that I would occasionally take point. I'm certain that if they had known, Lieutenant Webster and Doctor Pasker would not have sanctioned this. I knew the areas where a trip wire or an ambush would be most likely. I trusted my ability to keep us out of trouble, and I could use this as a teaching opportunity. I was really beginning to enjoy the fact that I had not needed to stop the bleeding from a wounded Marine in several days. One day before a patrol, some of these new guys started to talk among themselves. I could tell that their fears were going to become a big danger to them and to me. I rubbed the caduceus emblem that I wore on my hat in the sand until all the black paint wore off and the brass shone in the sun like a beacon. At this point, I reminded them that they were Marines, and it was not going to look very good to their buddies that some sailor was tougher than they were. Like I said, I was becoming uncivilized and more of a Marine than I would have anticipated. My psychology worked, and their training, confidence, and pride returned. They did respect that I had kept myself alive this long. Now I was one of the seasoned men with dirty boots, and they listened when I told them where and what to look for to avoid walking into traps.

At some point, it became necessary for the company intelligence officer to speak with the village elders. The big problem here was that the elders spoke no English and we had no translator. Finally, someone noticed that our Navy chaplain was standing off to the side engaged in conversation with the Vietnamese priest from the church. As luck would have it, they were both Catholic priests and were speaking in Latin. So with the help of the priests, the discussion went from English to Latin to Vietnamese and back. Harriet's mother, Aileen Myers, came to love this story since she was a high school Latin teacher. I included it in a letter home, and she shared it with all her students. When I took Latin in high school, we had a poem that went: Latin is a dead language. As dead as it can be. First, it killed the Romans. Now it's killing me.

Maybe not so much!

# A GOURMET'S GUIDE TO VIETNAM

It would be remiss of me not to include a section on the dietary delights of the combat soldier. C-rats is short for combat rations. If we are what we eat, this next section may be kind of frightening. All kidding aside, Uncle Sam tried to make sure that we had food to keep us healthy and strong, and while uncertain of how it would measure up to the dietary restrictions of today, low/high fat, high/low carbs, etc. it did provide the energy we required. The only downside was the monotony of the same meal choices that set in after the first two or three months. I have mentioned in earlier stories how we were able to spice things up at times and occasionally add some variation.

Each case contained twelve boxed meals; there was a thirteenth choice if they were packaged prior to 1945! This extra meal was ham and lima beans, affectionately dubbed ham and mother f—kers. The meals were in a cardboard box about three-by four-by six inches and weighed three to five pounds. They contained olive green cans with black letters to warn consumers of the contents. The main courses included spiced beef, beef stew, beans and meatballs, Beanie Weenies (canned baked beans with cut up hotdogs), spiced chicken, pork slices, ham slices, ham and eggs, turkey loaf, macaroni and cheese, spaghetti and meatballs, and spaghetti in sauce. The boxes also contained smaller tins filled with such items as crackers and an even smaller tin of peanut butter or jelly. There was also what we called John Wayne candy bars—two-inch circles of chocolate, a quarter inch thick, with or without nuts, fruitcake, which was the universal least favorite choice. Fruitcakes were hard and dry, and the only living thing that enjoyed them was Ricky Ticky the mongoose. There was also pound cake, sliced pears, sliced peaches, sliced apricots, fruit cocktail, and pineapple slices. Each meal contained a cellophane-wrapped plastic spork and knife, along with a brown foil packet, which contained small packets of salt, pepper, sugar, powered creamer, instant coffee, instant coco, a book of matches, four cigarettes of various brands, and a moistened hand wipe paper napkin. A small pack of toilet paper completed the contents of each meal box. In each case of twelve meals, there were usually a half dozen small can openers, nicknamed P-38s. I do not know why they were called P-38s. They were a small rectangle of metal, one and a half inches by three quarters of an inch; another piece of metal, half as long with the lower edge, curved and sharpened, was hinged so it lay flat until opened for use. P-38s would last about a month before being lost or wearing out, and we all carried two or three. The packing dates on most of our meals was in the 1940s and 1950s, so it would be safe to say that much of the time the food was older than the men eating it.

When supplies came in, we divided into groups of three or four, taking turns picking our meals from the case so the dirty boots did not scarf up all the choice selections. Some trading usually occurred as we took items out of their boxes and stowed them in our backpacks. The cardboard was buried or burned.

Everyone was very aware of weight that had to be carried, and ounces were shaved off wherever possible.

Along with the food, but packed separately, was a supply of sterno tablets, each individually wrapped in brown foil. Sterno tabs are a compressed, flammable, light blue fuel, about one by two by one half inches, used to heat our food. It gave off eye-watering, nose-burning fumes, so it was not a good idea to cook inside. Each "heat tab" would burn with a low blue flame for about five to ten minutes, and because it did not give off much light, we could make a cup of coffee in the bottom of a fighting hole. If you made friends with the combat engineers, an alternate source of heat C-4 (plastic explosive) was also available. It came in bars about one-by two-by ten inches and had the consistency of modeling clay. Sliced into thin wafers, it burned very hot and very fast. A hot cup of coffee could be ready in about a minute. The drawback here was the very bright light it emitted, thereby eliminating nighttime use. It was best to let it burn itself out, which it did in a hurry. A word of caution: never stomp on C-4 to put it out. You might get lucky and only lose the sole of your boot, but you could lose your soul.

A small, portable cook stove could be made using a cracker can; it was a bit bigger around than the meal cans. You removed one end and made a few holes in the side for air. If you were lucky, somebody had an old-fashioned beer can opener, the kind that makes triangular holes. You set your stove over a heat tab, placed your Beanie Weenies on top, and you were cooking supper. Meals were cooked in, and eaten out of, the can. We did not want the extra weight or the clatter of cookware, and doing dishes was easy. We simply buried them. C-rats kept you going but could not compare to care packages from home.

B-rations were mostly dehydrated foods packed in the same olive green cans, only larger. While the biggest C-ration was the size of a soup can, the smallest B-ration was closer to a three-pound coffee can. Inside were all kinds of fruits and vegetables, pasta, instant mashed potatoes, rice, bouillon, boneless chicken, pork chops, and steaks. You added a bit of water, soaked the contents through the night, and the next day you ate really great.

Long Range Patrol Rations (LRP) were the predecessor to today's Meals Ready to Eat (MRE). Much lighter to carry than C-rats, the main meals were dehydrated. There was chili, corned beef hash, pastas, and stews, as well as packs of trail mix/gorp, cookies, and cakes. The foil packs contained the same items as in C-rats, with the addition of Chiclets, Starburst, or Kraft Caramels. To prepare the meal, you heated water, poured it into the top of the plastic bag the food was in, waited at least five minutes for everything to rehydrate, and than ate. Unfortunately, the chili beans were always crunchy in the center, no matter how long you waited.

The ARVN and NVA rations were very similar to each other. The ARVN soldiers that traveled with us as scouts carried a couple of pounds of rice in plastic bags, some dried fish or other meat, and dehydrated vegetables. They would mix the various ingredients and cook it in a small saucepan. They also usually had fresh fruit. The ARVN also carried some C-rats and LRPs since they were receiving their supplies from us too.

Occasionally, when we were near a village, the people were grateful for the protection we provided and, to stay on our good side, would invite us to eat with them. The general rule of polite etiquette regarding the main course was that we did not ask and they did not tell. I always felt a little better if there were chickens around, but it was usually stew in a large community pot. It often tasted like rodents and was actually quite tasty. Ratatouille, anyone?

I am sure that people stationed in the supply and support back in the rear were tired and bored with the monotony of the chow hall food. But for those of us who had to carry around what we ate, any mess hall food meant fine dining. There you would receive a mix of fresh, canned, boxed, and packaged foods prepared from a recipe in pots and pans on a stove. The part of the meal that was supposed to be hot was hot, and the part that was to be cold was cold. The taste, of course, depended on the quality of the food and the quality of the cook. Word got around as to where the better places were, and the best of the best was the Navy Construction Battalion (CBees).

On Thanksgiving Day, they flew hot food in insulated containers out to us while we were still in the bush. The meal was mashed potatoes and gravy, corn, green beans, deboned turkey, and pineapple ice cream for dessert. By the time the food arrived, it was overcooked but still a tasty reminder of a holiday meal from home. Maybe it's just me, but it lost a little in the translation, especially with being able to drink the ice cream.

The last and best tasting supply of food was the stateside foods that came in our packages from home. I had written in my letters that the things we could carry easily and use the most were Kool-Aid and other powdered drink mixes, anything to kill the taste of the Halzone tablets we put in our water to help purify it. Cracker Jacks and Jiffy Pop popcorn were loved by all. Dry soup could be eaten as soup or added to C-rats to boost the flavor. Hard candy and any homemade desert, such as cookies, breads, or fudge, were devoured immediately. With no refrigeration and concerns about shipping weight, I know it was not easy for them to shop for us, but the folks back home did a wonderful job. They sent a very wide variety of very useable items.

## THE MESS HALL

One thing the combat infantry is always on the lookout for is real food, preferably served on plates and eaten while sitting at a table. Doc Keith Sieb was still with the platoon at the time of this story.

We had gotten back to a good-sized base camp after a fairly long and tiring mission and were looking forward to a hot meal of something other than C-rations. We located a large mess hall belonging to some unit (not ours) and joined the line of men waiting to go in and eat. The line was long, stretching out to and along the edge of the roadway. The line moved slowly.

Eventually, we approached a point where the sidewalk leading from the building met the road. Keith was talking with me and had his back to the line and sidewalk, unaware of the people coming down this walkway. The line moved forward a bit, and as he turned and took a step, he almost collided with a full bird Marine colonel.

"Excuse me, sir," Keith said.

"That's quite all right, Marine," the colonel replied.

"We are not Marines, sir. We are sailors," responded Keith.

"What outfit are you with?" the Bird asked, turning around.

"1/9, sir," we replied in unison.

"This is a 7th Marines mess hall," the colonel snapped. "You don't eat here."

We stepped out of line, thinking we had missed out on a hot meal. After the colonel moved off, the Marines in line invited us right back in. We made some new friends and had a good supper that night.

We had just returned to VCB from a major sweep and were back in the company area with a couple of days off from standing lines. Since some of our trucks had recently taken enemy fire, word was passed that a convoy headed south to Dong Ha needed some troops to ride "shotgun" (armed guard). Lieutenant Webster talked with us, and it was decided that we would go because the reward was a sit-down meal at a real chow hall. The trip was uneventful, which was probably very wise on the enemy's part because if they had messed with our dinner plans, we would have been as mean as snakes. Riding down Highway 9, on the top of a loaded 6 by 6, covers a person in a layer of dust. Mixed with the sweat of a ninety-degree day, we were soon covered head to toe with field fashionable mud. Add to that the fact that we had been several days in the field without a shower or bath. We were certainly a smelly and scruffy bunch.

The drivers dropped us off inside the gate at Dong Ha and gave the lieutenant directions to a nearby mess hall. We snapped on the safeties, unloaded our weapons, and moved out along the road. The building was huge and resembled an airplane hangar with a smaller building attached to one end, which was the officers' mess. We moved off to the side of the street, took off our gear and sat down, while Lieutenant Webster went up to obtain permission for us to have supper there. I watched the men standing in line with their shiny boots, crisply blocked hats, and their clean, freshly starched, and pressed jungle fatigues. Each man was carrying his own metal food tray, silverware, and cup. When Lieutenant Webster returned, he said they initially had not wanted to feed us. He told them he had eighteen hot, dusty, exhausted Marines waiting outside. They were fresh out of the bush and just off convoy duty and still packing live ammo. They were hungry and tired of eating C-rations. He was reasonably certain that if he had to go back outside and tell us men that we would not be fed here, what would be left of their mess hall would definitely leak during the next rainstorm. For some reason, they changed their minds. Lieutenant Webster would eat in the Officers' Mess, and we could use the main side. He also told us that everyone who usually ate here had their own eating gear, as I had observed, but they would round up the paper plates and plastic utensils. They had no cups—no big problem.

"Where's the dumpster?" I asked one of the men in line.

I took the guys around back, stuck my head in a dumpster, and came out holding empty cans with the lids still partially hooked on. When we each had a can, I took them over to the tray washing station. These consisted of three galvanized trashcans with a submersible heater in each can; they were full of very hot water. Number one had soap and water, with a couple of scrub brushes hanging on the side. Number two was used for the first rinse and number three for a final rinse. When the cans were clean, we bent the lids into handles, and with our new cups we joined the chow line.

What was a plain everyday meal to them was ambrosia to us. What surprised me was that as smelly and dirty as we were, the local troops were actually willing and even eager to share a table with us. The clean and starched types were known by many different names by those of us in the bush, office poges, rear echelon mother f—kers (REMFs), or Remington Raiders, after the brand of typewriter. Most of them had not and probably would not ever see any actual combat. The Remington Raiders began to ask us all kinds of questions about life out in the bush.

"What's it like out there, man?"

"How bad are things up in Leatherneck Square, etc?"

When one of my friends called me "Doc John," two of our shiny-booted tablemates asked, "Are you the Doc John from Charlie Company 1/9?"

"I am," I said.

One of the men left the table, and a few minutes later, several other guys came over to our table just to meet me.

"Your reputation precedes you, man," one guy said.

"It is an honor to meet you, man. You have status with us back in the rear," said another.

I still do not know what stories had been told about me or who had told them. I felt honored and a bit embarrassed by all the attention.

## NEW YEAR'S EVE 1969

On the last day of 1968, by some stroke of luck, C Company had the good fortune of being out of the bush and off lines. We were back in the battalion compound area, sleeping on cots in tents, staying dry, and relaxing a bit. During the day, I visited BAS and picked up medications and dressings to replace those that had been depleted while we had been out. I wrote a couple of letters home and went down to the shower tent. I returned in time for mail call and was able to read my letters in comfort. That night, AFVN was going to be broadcasting a football game, Dallas and somebody. Several of the men had gone to the PX and bought several cases of beer.

So I got to thinking that my general plan was to forget the war by getting drunk and listening to the game. It was a good plan, except that as a corpsman I was on call 24/7. Before completing my first beer, one of the men, who had started drinking much earlier in the day, became sick. I led him over to BAS where he could sleep it off under the watchful eye of the duty corpsman.

*Now back to my friends*, I thought. A couple of cold ones and the ball game, right? Nope! Somebody on his way back from the latrine tripped on a tent stake and lacerated a leg. Then it was back to BAS, where I cleaned the wound and assisted Doctor Pasker with the placing of twelve stitches. It was not a serious injury but a fairly big one.

Arriving back at the party, I found a couple of numbskulls in a fight. Both of them were too drunk to inflict much damage, so a little bit of cleaning and a few Band-Aids later, I sent them to separate corners to sleep it off. By the time I got back to my friends, they were all asleep or passed out, and the game was over. I found myself an unopened beer and sat down and wrote some letters home. I was all alone, too sober, and wide awake. When I finished the beer and my letter writing, I glanced out the tent door and watched the sun rise on 1969.

"Goooooooooooooooooood morning, Vietnam!" blared out of the radio.

As camp came to life around me, I drew in a deep breath and thought, "another day closer to going home."

## NOT MY DRUGS

I know that many people thought the men serving in Vietnam were all a bunch of drugged-up crazies. While some units may have experienced a high volume of drug use, I did not find that to be true with our unit. When we came out of the bush, someone might take up a collection and buy a few cases of beer to share. That was only if we did not have to stand lines. There were two local hard liquors: one was called Silver Fox, and I do not remember the name of the other. Both tasted like kerosene. I never developed a taste for either. With the exception of New Year's and R&R, we never did have the quantity needed to get too drunk. I only recall two times when anything of a more illegal nature occurred.

Marijuana was around, but only once was it an issue, and that was a day when command ordered a surprise inspection of everyone's gear. As with all "surprises" in the military, there was some lead time before it actually occurred. Suddenly I had four Marines, all FNGs assigned as reinforcements, standing at my bunker.

"Doc. You're the only one we trust."

They brought their plastic sandwich bags of pot for me to hold until the inspection was over.

"Are you all crazy? I can't be caught with this stuff any more than you!"

After all, I was going to be inspected too. I took it from them and buried it on the hillside above our lines.

The inspection entailed laying the contents of our packs and pockets on top of our ponchos. The poor sergeant assigned to inspect my gear took a look at what I had laid out in front of me. I had my pack and one medical bag. My inspection took longer than the others because I carried so many small containers and packages. He finally completed going through this much and began to move onto the next man.

"Hold on, Sergeant. That was all I had room for in the allotted space," I said.

Putting away that which he had already inspected, I began to spread out the remaining supplies from my satchel bags and Unit 1. His face dropped because he knew he was going to be a long time going through all my pill bottles, etc. He decided to shorten the process.

"Do you have any drugs, Doc?"

"Yes, that's what I do."

"No. I mean narcotics."

"I have my morphine and pain pills."

I always jokingly said I carried enough morphine to calm down an angry water buffalo that is assuming I wanted to get close enough to give it to him. I had to play it a little dumb since this inspection was a "surprise."

"Doc, do you have any pot?" he finally asked.

"Oh! Is that what you are looking for? No, Sergeant, I do not. With the quantity and quality of what I carry, pot seems unnecessary."

He nodded and moved onto the next man. I packed my stuff.

The inspection was over. Nobody had anything; there was no reason to get anyone in trouble. I sort of forgot to mention the incident, except to the guys that needed to be clear thinking enough to be keeping me alive. I told them they could do what they wanted on their own time, but when we were in the bush or standing lines, I would not tolerate anyone being stoned and neither would the Marine Corps.

The second time was also a nonincident, as it turned out. It occurred as I was sitting alone writing a letter after a very rough mission. I heard the footsteps of about six men coming up behind me.

"Hey, Doc! Give us your morphine, man."

A morphine serret looks like a small tube of toothpaste, about one inch long, with a harpoon of a needle on the top (twenty gauge by one and a half inches long). I usually carried ten, and, like my seventh canteen, they were only for the wounded.

"You have got to be kidding. No! You are not getting my morphine."

Metal slid on metal behind me as at least two M-16s chambered rounds. Without saying a word, I reached into my pack and took out a small metal tin, the size of an Altoids mints box, and placed it on my cot. As one of them picked it up, I spoke very calmly, "I will not replace any of my supply that is used like this. Take a good look at the man next to you. He is your friend, and if he gets shot out there, I hope you have a really great time because there will not be any painkiller for him."

I did not even bother to say, "If you get shot," because no one believes they might catch a bullet. But they would worry about their buddies. They left with my tin.

Half an hour later, I heard the sound of three sets of boots walking up behind me. I did not turn and just kept on working on my letter. My morphine tin was dropped back on the cot beside me. I picked it up and placed it back into my pack without opening it.

"Thanks, guys. Oh, and by the way," I spoke in a very matter-of-fact voice.

"Don't you ever lock and load on me again because somebody won't be walking away from the situation if you do, and I have no intention of going home in a box."

Like I said, it was like living in the "wild west" at times. Only after they had gone did I pull the tin back out and check inside. All ten doses were still intact. I cannot say if it was their conscience or that big, harpoon-sized needle that stopped them. I was hoping that the manner in which it was handled would spread through the platoon, and I would never have to deal with a moment of temporary stupidity like this in the future. I did not report the incident. As I said before, Marines and their docs are as close as brothers, and we looked out for each other.

# III

## DEWEY CANYON AKA THE A SHAU VALLEY

I t was January 1969. I had voted in my first election while sitting atop a pile of sandbags that protected our fighting bunker. I had traveled literally halfway around the world, had climbed mountains, and had done more things physically and emotionally than I could have ever imagined. I had witnessed the death of some fine young men and had been, in part, responsible for saving the lives of many others. Up to this point, if a wounded Marine had been breathing when I got to him, he was still breathing when I put him aboard the dust-off and survived to go home. I had seen some of the worst of what humans could do to each other, but I had also witnessed real acts of courage, bravery, heroism, and the compassion that demonstrated the best humankind was capable of.

On one of our previous operations, we had been placed on twenty-four-hour standby. It seemed that Egypt and Israel were going head-to-head in the Middle East, and there was a real possibility that some dingbat politician was going to pull us out of our nice, comfortable war in the jungle and send us off to a brand new war in the desert. Man, did that sound crazy! Just when I was certain that there was no way things could be any worse, along came Operation Dewey Canyon.

The NVA had launched a major spring offensive in 1968 on Tet, the Asian new year, and had done a great deal of damage all over the country before they were driven back. All signs indicated that they would try again this year. Air reconnaissance, sound detectors, and several other intelligence-gathering sources indicated that the NVA were moving troops, supplies, and tanks down the Ho Chi Minh Trail. The trail was a vast network of roads and footpaths that cut through the jungle in Laos, Cambodia, and Vietnam, and it was constantly being improved. The road had been extended, widened, and hard-packed further and further south each month and was now able to support vehicular traffic. The NVA would drive through the night and, during the day, park in tree-covered areas. They would place potted trees or camouflaged netting on the roadways so our aircraft could not easily see it.

This year, we would not wait to meet the enemy when and where he picked but would take away his supplies and engage him at a time and place of our choosing. That time was now, and the place was the A Shau Valley. Prior to this, there had been little allied activity in this region, which consisted of thick jungle and formidable mountains bordering Laos and Cambodia. The NVA had been able to feel relatively safe there, but that was about to change dramatically.

It was a very well-thought-out operation, based on the classic "hammer-and-anvil plan" with a few embellishments. The anvil would consist of fire support bases and Marines surrounding the valley on the ridgelines. The hammer was the 9th Marines; 2/9 pushed up the right flank; 3/9 was on the left flank; and 1/9 would go right up the middle. Our job was to push the enemy toward the other units, and when the hammer and anvil met, anything in the middle would be destroyed. Large amounts of supplies were moved into VCB and made ready while both land and carrier-based air support were also put in place to support us.

Through the month of January, we were standing lines around VCB, while sites for fire support bases were being prepared and manned. Quite a few new men were being assigned to us, as our numbers had been depleted by men rotating out at the end of their tours and by the casualties from previous missions. Our numbers needed to return to near-full strength before starting this mission. We filled our days integrating new people into the unit, reading, writing letters, and keeping our weapons clean and ready. We were getting a much-needed rest and waiting for what lay ahead. We would pass the time playing cards and listening to the radio. We had a group of African American Marines that could sing as well as they could fight, and they would have impromptu a cappella concerts. These guys sang several songs and did a version of "Under the Boardwalk" that would blow you away. They had over a dozen songs they had practiced and, in a different time and place, would have most certainly gotten a recording contract. I continued to distribute malaria pills and made walking rounds every morning. I made my reports to Lieutenant Webster regarding the general health and condition of the troops. With rest and chow, our mental and physical condition was getting better every day.

Among the new additions was a new corpsman. Doc Paul was a lanky kid from Florida, and I started his orientation right away. I do not remember exactly who made the choice but, after just a few days, he was bumped to the company headquarters group. Perhaps it was my resolute refusal to leave the guys in light of the pending operation, which resulted in him being moved instead of me. Whatever the case, it was a good decision. He did a good job and fit in well there. A bit later in the operation, he was still available to help me when the things became really hairy.

We received daily reports and heard rumors on the progress of our brothers out in the bush. They were working around the clock, carving fire support bases out of the jungle, and securing their positions around the A Shau. They were already making enemy contact and finding stashes of supplies. We experienced a mixture of emotions. We felt both relief for our relative safety and guilt that we were not out in the bush helping them. There was also a trace of envy that they were getting all the glory, such as it was. But that too would change soon enough, because even though the brass was very tight-lipped about what was coming, we could sense that it was something very big.

After a couple of weeks of line standing and quiet patrols, we all felt rested and healthy. On February 11, word came from command to get ready to turn the lines over to our relief and saddle up on the landing zone. This was a bigger troop movement than the one going into the DMZ. The Sea Knights would land ten to twelve at a time; we were positioned along both sides of the strip in one-helicopter-load-sized groups. We were all fully loaded with our own gear, and each man was packing extra mortar rounds or an ammo box. As far as I could see, there were more helicopters coming in. As soon as one group landed and took on their load, the next group was coming in. Then it was our turn. We were all packing extra food and ammo and struggled a bit just to stand up and run onto the back of a waiting bird. We were soon airborne. I watched out of the door as VCB slipped into the distance. We all had butterflies churning in our bellies.

At the other end of our ride, the LZ scene was almost the same with the exception that men were now running off and clearing the zone for the next flight. Since it was a three-pronged assault, the number of flights was reduced at each LZ. We were set down in at least three different zones. We quickly moved out about three hundred meters along the ridgeline and set in our defensive positions for the night.

It was a good thing we were rested because there was little sleep that night. The NVA wasted no time in testing our perimeter. We received RPG rounds and grenades as well as some rifle fire before the night was over, but we made it through the night with no one injured. The new troops were still not sure what to make of this, and those of us who had "been there" before were steeling into our staying alive mode. At first light, we sent a team out in front of the lines to assess for battle damage. Several blood trails from wounded or killed NVA attackers were found going back downhill. They now knew this was not going to be easy for them either.

After eating breakfast, 1/9 moved out to begin our push. 2/9 and 3/9 did the same from their positions. We moved in a battalion-sized unit, alternating which company and which platoon took the point. It was not long before we started to find bunkers with small stores of food, equipment, and weapons. It was also not long before we started receiving and returning fire. Every day we had an objective to reach, and each evening we would dig in at that place. To decrease the chances of being marked by the enemy, we waited until dusk to send out one or two listening posts (LP) and/or an ambush fifty to one hundred meters in front of the lines. They had a radio and would check in every hour or sooner if something happened. I shared watch with the platoon radiomen. There were two RTOs so we had a three-man watch schedule. It was our job to stay in communication with the lookouts. They would keep their radio on very low, so as not to be overheard, which could give away their position. The communication would go like this: "Charlie 2 Lima Papa, Charlie 2 Squid. Sit Rep (situation report)."

They would then depress the talk button on their radio twice. "Kush, kush."

If all was well, I would hear the two quiet bursts of static and respond, "Roger Charlie 2 Lima Papa, I understand Sit Rep all clear."

"Charlie 2 Alpha, Charlie 2 Squid. Sit Rep."

"Kush, kush."

"Roger 2 Alpha, understand Sit Rep all clear." Every so often, I would add, "Stay alert out there, guys."

Then with our second radio, which was set on the company frequency, we would communicate, "Charlie actual, Charlie 2, all Sit Reps report normal."

That same process was being repeated every hour by every platoon that had people out in front. If they did see or hear something, they would radio it in at once, and we would go on full alert. Whispered orders were passed between each fighting hole, and everybody was awake and listening and watching into the blackness of night. Sometimes, the forward positions would fire on the enemy and then either change locations or come in. This was risky business in the dark. The best thing for them to do was to use hand grenades and Claymore mines, so the muzzle flashes from their rifles would not give away their position. Shortly after daybreak, the LPs and ambush teams would come back in. Claymore mines were defused and put back into the packs. Breakfast was eaten, and we would move out toward our next objective.

Claymores are anti-personnel mines, also called half moon mines, because of their curved shape. They are a portable, defensive, explosive device, a foot long, six inches wide, and an inch and a half thick, with a hinged metal stake on each corner, used to hold them in place. They are slightly curved plastic boxes, which contained a large slab of C-4 plastic explosive. In front of the C-4 are approximately two hundred ball bearings. A blasting cap attached to two wires is inserted into a hole at the base of the box. At the other end of the wires there was a Marine with a small box about the size of a cigarette pack. This was the trigger. Claymores were placed, curved side out, with something solid, like a tree or rock, behind them because even though most of the blast went forward, pieces from the back of the case went in all directions. It was also a good idea to camouflage them since a very quiet and well-trained enemy solider could find them and, before making his attack, would have it turned around so that, when triggered, the ball bearings would be coming straight back at us. That would be a very bad way to start off a battle.

# CASUALTIES OF WAR

On February 13, we had point, and my old friend Hobo was up front. As with most of the days, it was hot and humid. The morning march had been quiet, and around midday we were moving up the side of yet another mountain. I was looking forward to being back on the high ground because usually there was a breeze and the humidity was not as bad. You may recall that we had picked up several new people in the platoon while back at VCB. Two of them, PFC Naylor and PFC Day, were childhood friends that had grown up in the same San Diego neighborhood. They had enlisted on the buddy system and had gone through boot camp and advanced infantry training (AIT) together. Both were assigned to Second Platoon Charlie Company 1/9. The trail brought us up out of the trees and along the side of a gentler ridge. I was about the tenth in line, and as I cleared the tree cover, I was grateful to feel the breeze on my face.

*Clack, clack, clack.*

Suddenly, the distinctive chatter of AK-47 fire broke the silence. As I hit the ground and looked for cover, I saw PFC Naylor fall. Just two men in front of me, he was now lying in the open on the steep slope, just off the trail, and exposed to the direction of the enemy fire. I was instantly back on my feet and moving toward him. Quickly reaching him, I pulled him up to trail level and into a very handy shallow depression and started to assess his wounds. He was unconscious, and both his trouser legs were full of blood. We all kept our trouser cuffs tied at the ankles to keep leeches out. Using my K-Bar knife, I slit his trousers and found his wounds. To stop the bleeding, I applied tight battle dressings to the entry and exit wounds on the left thigh and then did the same to the right. He had lost a lot of blood; I was attempting to set up an IV line to get some fluids on board. Then he stopped breathing. As I did two cycles of mouth-to-mouth breathing and chest compressions, I could hear the rapid fire of M-16s around me. Then I completed the placement of the IV line, and with fluids going wide open, I went back to my resuscitation efforts. The firefight was over now, and Sergeant Christensen came over and put his hand on my shoulder.

"Doc, you have six wounded over here that need you."

Damn it! I hate triage. I knew from the location of the wounds and the amount of blood loss that a single bullet had most likely severed femoral veins and arteries in both legs. These blood vessels are about the size of your thumb. Even if I stayed with him, he did not have a chance. He had lost too much blood in the first fifteen to thirty seconds before I even got to him. I left him with a Marine who held his head and comforted him. He never regained consciousness. I collected my gear and moved up the trail. The wounded had all been brought to a sheltered spot, so I assessed the severity of their wounds and began treatment. At one point, I looked over to see Doc Paul and Doc Sieb, who had moved up through the lines to give me a hand. From the look of things, they had found a few casualties along the way.

My most stable patient, and the last to have his wound dressed, was Hobo, who had stood by patiently while I treated his handler. Hobo's wound was an "in and out" on his right front shoulder with no broken bone. By the time our Sea Knight dust-off arrived, all the wounded were stable. Since we had no level spot for an LZ, the pilot backed his helicopter up to the slope, the angle of the mountainside matching his raised ramp. With his ramp resting on the ground and nose in the air, he held the Sea Knight level in a fantastic hover. We loaded our one dead and several wounded comrades on board. We were very careful of the tail rotor, which was dangerously close to the ground. Once again, that pilot was Mike Bertalon.

Years later when we were talking, Mike remembered that day. My gentle dog friend Hobo had wandered up into the cockpit with growls and bared teeth.

"I was not sure if he wanted to take over the flying or was just telling me to get them out of there safely," Mike said.

Then he assured me that all of the wounded had made it back to the hospital and that Hobo, after his brief visit in the cockpit, had stuck like glue to Ron, his handler, the entire flight back.

We did not move much farther that day since the ridgeline we were on was our objective. We set our perimeter and were digging in when we heard the *bloop, bloop* sound of mortars being fired.

"Incoming!" someone shouted.

Everyone took cover and began looking for the NVA mortar crew. If they could see us, we might be able to see them. As always, the explosion of incoming rounds soon occurred. My hand was resting on my gear. I awaited that call I knew so well. Sure enough, it came.

"Pig Pen up!"

I ran toward the call. I never knew exactly what I would find when I got there. Sometimes, it was an easy fix of a relatively minor wound, but not today. I arrived to find that a mortar round had landed in an occupied foxhole.

"Oh shit!" I said when I saw who he was.

What are the odds? I had one dead and one seriously wounded. Pulling them from the hole with the help of another man, I went to work. Applying battle dressings, I was able to stop the bleeding and stabilize the wounded man. The concussion injuries would have to be addressed on the *USS Repose*. It was getting late, but there was still enough daylight left to get them both out on a dust-off.

My adrenaline level was returning to normal as I watched the medivac chopper grow smaller in the blue sky. I took a deep breath and thought of the tragic irony of the situation that had just occurred. The young Marine that was killed in the foxhole was PFC Day.

There was an expended LAW, a kind of disposable bazooka, beside the foxhole. I like to think that Day got off a shot and took out the mortar and crew, killing the NVA soldiers that shot both Naylor and himself, thus closing the circle of the tragedy. The two young friends from San Diego who had indeed done everything together. Sitting down on a rock, I lit a cigarette.

"What a crappy day it's going to be in that neighborhood next week," I said aloud to no one.

## THE GOONEY BIRDS

The next day found us moving up the ridge with Alpha Company out on point. Their lead elements tripped a booby trap, wounding two men. A bit farther down the trail, they spotted an ambush waiting for them. They were able to strike first, killing or wounding several of the enemy in the ensuing firefight. Bravo Company was next, followed by H&S Company (Headquarters and Supply), then Charlie Company. We were all taking sniper fire and mortar rounds. All this activity made for very slow going, but eventually, the pace picked up. That night, we dug our holes a little deeper. We were very alert.

Throughout the night, we detected movement all around the lines. We called in for a fixed-wing gunship for close air support. These propeller-driven twin-engine aircraft had at least four mini-guns mounted on the sides with call names like Spooky and Puff the Magic Dragon. They flew much slower than a jet and were able to make tight circles in the air above us, providing air cover by shooting with accuracy as close as ten yards in front of us. With Spooky overhead, each fighting position lit a sterno tablet and placed it in the bottom of their hole. There was not enough light for the enemy to see us, but from the sky above the gunners could easily mark our perimeter by connecting the light blue dots. They opened fire. The ominous roar of the mini-guns sounded like a hundred chainsaws, but the truly awesome thing was the sight of a wide tube of red fire coming from the sky. Every fifth round was a tracer that glowed red as it traveled from the gun to the ground. There was so much firepower that it appeared to be four solid reddish-yellow ribbons coming from above, each about two feet wide. Watching these columns of fire, I could only think how much they resembled water pouring from a hose. When the guns opened fire, they could put a bullet in every square foot of an area the size of a football field in under three seconds. A football field is forty yards wide and one hundred yards long and equals 36,000 square feet. They worked the area around us for a good twenty to thirty minutes, which is a lot of three seconds. The early morning patrols found over two dozen blood trails from injured or killed NVA soldiers leading away from our lines.

# LEFT BEHIND

The next day was hot and sultry and again found us bringing up the rear. We were on the move when the call, "Corpsman up, heat casualty," was passed man to man until it reached me. I picked up my pace and began to pass the men ahead of me, looking for the downed Marine. I must have passed about thirty men as we continued to move uphill. I still had not found the affected man. The increased effort was making me feel as if I would be the next heat casualty. I came upon a man I recognized as a corpsman from the Third Platoon. I asked him if he had heard a "corpsman up" call, but he was not aware of it. I was now overheated and ticked off. Deciding not to walk back down the path just to have to come back up, I moved off to the side into some shade and waited for the Second Platoon to catch up with me. I was now quite a way in front of them.

Then the line of men stopped moving. Ten or fifteen minutes passed, and we were still not moving. Most of the Third Platoon had gone past, so my guys must be close. Having cooled down, I took a salt tab, and a drink, and decided to move back down the trail to join them. Moving in combat patrol, we usually kept five to ten yards between each man, so after passing six to eight men, I had covered about fifty yards. I was approaching the last man in the Third Platoon, who was not covering to the side of the line but was watching straight back.

"Where ya going, Doc?"

It was then that I discovered that the whole Second Platoon had left me and pulled back to the previous night's camp to act as a rear guard and set up an ambush. They had a good fifteen- to twenty-minute head start on me, and you can bet your sweet bippy I had no plans to walk back through the jungle alone. These guys were not going to help me with an escort, so I moved back up the line until I found a radioman.

"Hey, man, can I use your radio?"

"Sure, Doc!"

"Charlie 2, Charlie 2, this is Charlie 2 Squid. Over."

"Go ahead 2 Squid. Over."

"Charlie 2, be advised you left without me. Over."

After a pause, "Pigpen, 6 says come on down. Over."

"Tell 6 to send back a fire team to keep me company, and I will be happy to. Over."

In retrospect, this was a scary thought that I would be willing to walk through almost a click of enemy-infested jungle with only four other people. I had been with the Marines too long. Another pause.

"6 says it's secure. Just come on down. Over."

"Charlie 2, if that's not a direct order and there is not going to be any escort, I'm not walking back alone, and be advised I will be spending the night with the neighbors. Over." Pause.

"Pigpen, 6 says it's your call. Over."

Now I paused a minute to consider my options. Remember that fine line between bravery and stupidity? The idea of a casual stroll by myself, in this situation, crossed that line. By making the choice mine, Lieutenant Webster had not given me a direct order.

"Charlie 2, I will see you in the morning. Please stay out of trouble down there.

Pigpen out."

With that, I moved up and found the Third Platoon's lieutenant and let him know that I would be spending the night with them. I also found the reason things had slowed down to such a slow pace. There was a spot in our line of progress that went almost straight up about thirty feet and had to be climbed using ropes. I took my turn, and once over this spot, I soon reached the night's position. I dug a nice deep hole and ate supper with the battalion's chaplain. He did not come out into the bush too often, but on a full battalion mission like this one, he was right there. Gutsy, when you consider he too was a displaced sailor attached to the Marines. The night was quiet on all fronts, and by 0900 hours, the Second Platoon had joined up with the main body. I was greatly relieved, because I had worried about them all night.

## KEEPING THE PRESSURE ON

For the next couple of days, we moved up and down mountains in the hot, humid weather. During my daily malaria pill rounds, I kept a close check on the condition, both physical and mental, of my troops. It had been raining a lot, and several of the men were developing jungle rot on their feet and ankles. We also took some incoming fire every day—RPGs, mortars, AK-47s, or all of the above. At night, we dug in and took more attacks, all of which we pushed back. The men were holding up well, considering the conditions. I made sure Lieutenant Webster was kept updated on these matters.

The NVA appeared to be consistently pulling back into our trap, and we were dealing with their rear guard. They were fighting a game of hit and move to give their command personnel time to get away. In the process, they left a lot of supplies in their wake. We were pushing hard, and they were feeling the pressure. This became very clear when one day we came upon a good-sized, abandoned base camp. It looked like Headquarters and Supply for at least a battalion, maybe even a regiment, and they had left in a big hurry. Among the food, weapons, personal gear, and ammunition, we also found several documents that we forwarded to our S2 intelligence section. In this camp, we found solid evidence: clothing, a helmet, and papers of a Russian military adviser. A marine brought me a backpack that probably had belonged to an NVA Doc. I looked through it and found several old French battle dressings, gauze wraps, and, most importantly, a plastic bottle filled with liquid soap. All of it became a part of my diminishing supplies. The soap smelled medicated. A little later, I would do a test and clean off one small area of jungle rot on my ankle. Jungle rot was our name for a nasty fungal infection of the skin, which developed where wet clothing chafed the skin. The soap worked great. The spot I treated was significantly better by the next morning. In the backpack, I also found a journal with the photos of two Vietnamese ladies tucked inside. One was an older woman, whom I took to be a mother, and the second an attractive young woman, who I guessed was a wife or sweetheart. As I sat and looked at his personal gear, I thought this young man was not so unlike me. I took a couple of extra minutes and repacked his backpack with his purely personal items. I placed his journal in a plastic bag and tucked the whole thing in a sheltered hollow in a big rock. I hoped that it would eventually get back to its rightful owner or to his family.

When we came upon such large amounts of abandoned supplies, we had to slow down a little and do something with them. If we just continued to move ahead, the NVA would come along behind us and pick up their supplies, and we would have gained nothing. Bags of rice and other foods were lifted out by helicopter and taken to the local people who had been displaced by the fighting. They were living in camps that had been built as safe shelters away from the fighting. War supplies were destroyed on site with explosives. Our combat engineers were constantly asking to have more C-4 sent out since we were finding so many supplies. Our Sea Knights were kept very busy, bringing out supplies for us and taking back captured food. When all was cleared, we could move on again.

The main body of the battalion continued to push the enemy, leaving the Second Platoon to provide security as the cache was cleaned out. This took the rest of the day and part of the next. Once the job was completed, we saddled up and set out to catch up with the main force. As a smaller unit, we could move faster and planned to catch up in about two days.

## DOWN BY THE RIVERSIDE

We were now moving along a part of the Ho Chi Minh Trail, beneath a canopy of old growth tropical forest. It was amazingly beautiful. Most of the tree trunks were over six feet in diameter and extended upward of fifty feet or more before any branches or leaves sprouted from their sides. The ground was clear of vegetation except for the occasional spot where a bomb or natural event, like a storm, had broken its limbs. This created a hole in the canopy, which was easily over one hundred feet above us. In those spots, the earth had quickly sprouted new plants such as wild flowers and vines. Much of the ground here had not seen sunshine in decades, and I was amazed at how quickly the seemingly sterile ground had come back to life.

We were following a footpath that was a part of the route over which supplies and troops could and did move unseen from the aircraft above. The trail was hard-packed and well defined, and where it went over steep grades, stairways, and handrails, it had been constructed from natural materials. These went on for miles. The builders of this massive maze of trails had spent a lot of time and energy, and I could not help but admire their tenacity and ingenuity.

Eventually, we were down in a valley moving parallel to a river that was the width of a two-lane street. Judging from the blackish green color of the water, it was quite deep. The trees were smaller and less thick in this area, so the ground cover was much more abundant and grew right down to the water's edge. The trail was similar to many I had walked along as a boy while trout fishing with my father. I wondered if there were trout in Southeast Asia. At one point, our trail crossed a shallow feeder stream where the three- to four-inch deep clear water tumbled and gurgled over the stony bottom, creating a thirty to forty foot open area. We were moving along quietly in combat spread, and six or eight of us had crossed this spot when *we* heard *Clack, clack, clack.*

The NVA sprang their ambush. We hit the ground and returned fire. Through the din of M-16, AK-47, M-60 fire, and occasional RPG and grenade explosions, I heard the call of a wounded Marine. Then I heard another. They were back down the trail on the other side of the wide-open stream crossing. *Where else would it be?* I thought. That crossing spot was now in the center of the ambush.

I had about fifty feet to cover before coming to the open area. Enough time and space to build up a good head of steam. As I popped out into the clearing, I was moving as fast as I could. A little over halfway across, my foot found the slippery rock and my body arched straight upward. Time switched into slow motion.

"Oh crap! I'm either going to fall on these rocks and break my fool neck, get shot, or both."

Swinging one of my satchel packs in a wide arc, I somehow managed to keep my balance with just a little loss of forward momentum. Making it to the other side still in one piece, I was soon busy treating the wounded as the fight continued. There were two arm wounds, one with a broken bone and one leg wound that, thankfully, missed the bone and major blood vessels. These were standard bullet or fragment wounds; all would be walking wounded for us once the battle dressings were secured. Through the clamor of gunfire, I heard sounds coming from across the river that indicated to me that the enemy had suffered at least twice our number of casualties. The depth of the river and not knowing the size of the opposing force prevented any recon of the opposite bank, so we carefully moved forward and found a place where we could call in a dust-off.

While waiting for the evacuation of our wounded, I gave my own gear a good inspection. In the satchel bag that had helped me stay upright were the broken remains of one of four IV bottles. It must have hit a rock when I slipped earlier since I did not find any bullet holes. My camera had also been in this bag, and the lens was now sealed shut by dried salt and sugar crystals from the dextrose and saline. Later on, when that roll of film was developed, telltale spots peppered the pictures, a permanent reminder of that day. With our wounded on their way to the next level of care, we moved on toward our night position.

## WHERE PURGATORY MEETS PARADISE

We were off the trail, not wanting to be easy pickings for another ambush, and moving uphill under the forest canopy. Up ahead, sunlight filtering through the trees to the ground indicated that we were approaching a clearing. It was late afternoon; we were weary and footsore as we walked into the blazing sunshine.

I stood on the raw edge, a place where total chaos melds with awe-inspiring beauty. I was on the top of a mountain, a panoramic view stretching out before me. Mountains, ridges, and valleys, all covered in a smooth, undulating jungle canopy that displayed every hue and shade of green. Above was a magnificent sky, the definitive sky blue, with just a few stark white fluffy clouds scattered about. Of course, my camera was broken.

Of all the places we had been so far, this one small piece of Vietnam's real estate hit me deep in my core. This was a place where I really did consider that I might one day be writing down these stories. I had barely passed English Composition in college. I longed for the artistic talent of a writer. How could an ordinary soldier find the words to describe cotton ball clouds, whiter than snow, drifting so close I felt I could almost touch them? The unspoiled beauty of the green carpet far below me, where in at least two places waterfalls cascaded down through hundreds of feet of lush green foliage, the stark white of their rolling mist so vivid that I could sense their calm, their coolness. My eyes caught sight of random clusters of orchids and wildflowers for which I had no names in the treetops surrounding the clearing. Because of the sloping ground, they were now at eye level.

Moving forward, I found myself in the center of a circular area with a fifty-yard diameter. The proud mountain had once been beautiful. Now the earth beneath my feet had been turned, churned, and mixed multiple times by the impact of bombs and artillery shells. Rocks had been smashed and thrown around so often that there were very few larger than a basketball, and the land was pocked with craters within craters. Everything was a light gray color, the dust of this once proud peak. The few stark tree trunks that were still recognizable were shattered and splintered from the shrapnel and flying soil that had once given them life. Now those few that were not lying in bits on the ground resolutely stood at unnatural angles and were coated in the same monotone gray giving the whole scene an eerie lunar feeling. No birds, no bugs, just silence with the volume turned way up. Amidst this great open wound, this place looked to be about as close to absolute destruction as I could imagine.

We had, with our wondrous ability to mess things up, insulted the earth, and we were not done yet. A good distance down the valley, I could see the F-4 Phantoms dropping napalm. It was so out of place, the bright orange and red fireballs literally flowing across the tops of the trees. Thick black smoke billowed upwards. Perhaps it was my Potawatomie heritage, the lessons of respect for the land taught to me by my father and grandfather, that at that moment made me pray for this madness to stop.


We stopped there for the night. I made my line check and then opened an olive green can of spiced ham and another of pineapple slices. I could not shake the feelings that had touched me so deeply on this day. It would take years for me to understand the surreal connection I felt in the bleakness of my own situation. How could these worlds be so inclusive of each other? How could the utter devastation where I sat coexist with the serenity upon which I gazed? For many years, I carried that image in my heart before understanding came to me. That place has become a metaphor to me. Our young lives were the unspoiled land, and the brutal devastation of Vietnam that daily attacked our senses was the open wound on our psyche. For many, the new growth would come and heal over the scar, and they would move on. For some, the wounds would fester, and they would endure the pain for the rest of their days.

The monsoon season was officially over, but on that night an unusual weather pattern moved in and we had the uncommon pleasure of being subjected to a cold rain, yet again. I dug down into the very bottom of my pack and found my olive green sweatshirt that usually served as a reasonably soft pillow. This was one of only four or five times when I was really glad I carried that thing around. It was going to be another one of those high-ranking nights on the miserable list. I stood watch with the radiomen that night. I even stayed awake an extra hour because the man on watch got to stay in the middle, with a warm person on either side. We moved out at first light and caught up with the rest of the battalion by midday.

# BOO COO BUSY DAY

Like every other day on this operation, we had not stayed in any one place for long. At daybreak, after a quick bite to eat, we continued our mission. This particular branch of the trail followed the top of the ridgeline. The Second Platoon was again in line for point and was going at a steady pace. We had come to a saddle where the ridge narrowed to about one hundred feet of gently rounded terrain. The very steep drops on either side created a perfect site for an ambush. We slowed the pace and moved cautiously forward.

Suddenly, the shooting started, and we spread out in a line across the top of the ridge, facing a similar line of NVA soldiers about fifteen yards away. This was not your usual hit-and-run firefight; we were involved in a serious head-to-head battle with an enemy who were dug in and determined to protect something. To the rear, our mortar teams were set up and were able to lay down some very effective fire at very close quarters. Along with rifle fire, grenades, and RPGs, both sides had machine guns menacingly chattering their lethal sweeps. Chuck and Craig, our M-60 machine gunners were laying down heavy return fire. I think they were tired of lugging ammo around and wanted to lighten their loads in a way that would do the most good.

Over the next twenty to forty minutes, there were multiple casualties on both sides. Oddly, every other man along my side was wounded, and unfortunately for me, it was one to the right, then to the center, then back to the right, then to the left. I was about five to ten yards in back of our line using all the cover I could find, which was not much, as I ran back and forth across the open area on the crest. I was finishing up with a dressing on an arm when I heard another call for help from my right. I stopped behind a small rise, just above the wounded man. Bullets were impacting the dirt between us with the steadiness of raindrops. The wounded guy was one of three men who were using a large log for protection. I steeled myself and was about to break cover when one of them shouted:

"Don't come down here, Pig Pen! You will only get pinned down. You can't help him anyway."

"Are you absolutely sure?"

"Yeah, man! He's been hit right in the forehead. He's f—king dead."

He flipped back the guy's helmet, and I could see the lethal wound. The man was Chuck; he had quickly become a good buddy of Doc Paul and was one member of my favorite fire team of practical jokers. I knew it was going to be a tough loss for Doc Paul.

Another call came from behind and to my right. No time to dwell on this now, it was back to business. It was Trigger, a skinny kid with a mop of black hair. He was alert and talking (not what I was used to finding) and was more angry than hurt when I got to him.

"Where you hit?"

"I can't tell you."

"What! Come on, man, are you hit or not?"

"They shot me in the ass, Doc!"

Sure enough, he had an in-and-out wound through the muscle of his left buttock. He was worried that I would think he was running away, but the entrance wound indicated he was facing the enemy. By now, Doc Paul and Doc Sieb had both come up from the back of the line. Both were busy with the wounded on the left side of our line. I was securing the last knot on Trigger's battle dressing and thinking how grateful I was for the help when the ground shook with another grenade explosion.

"I got the machine gun. I got the machine—Aiehhhh! I've been shot in the leg."

It was Lance Corporal Latane, one of our Native American scouts. He was on my right and fairly far forward. Knowing that Doc Paul, Doc Sieb, and probably one or two others were now busy at work helping me, I pointed at two nearby Marines, both of whom had only recently joined us in the field.

"Come on! I need cover! We are going after Latane!"

He continued to yell, and I kept crawling toward his voice, thinking I had fire support behind me. I noticed a subtle change in the sounds of the fight as I moved forward. The rounds whizzing above me were now from the rear. Somehow, I had gotten through the NVA line undetected and could now see my guy. I was beginning to have confidence that this was going to work out, but when I looked back to give direction to my escorts, they were nowhere to be found. FNGs! No time to worry about that now. I had come this far, and I could not leave him. He was still shouting when I reached him.

"Doc! My leg hurts!"

"Shut up, man! I'm here."

"It hurts. I need some morphine."

"Shut the f—k up before every gook in the valley knows where we are!"

I dressed and splinted his leg, and all the while, he was asking for morphine and I was growling in a low voice for him to keep quiet. With the leg stable, I dug in my pack and withdrew a tube of morphine. With the plastic cap in my teeth, I pushed the stylus in to break the seal and threw it aside. I plunged the needle through his trousers into his uninjured thigh, and squeezed the tube, injecting the medicine. His only response was to yell again that he didn't get the shot. Out of frustration, I pulled out my K-Bar. His eyes widened as I slit the leg of his trousers.

"You see that tiny little hole right there? Well, that is where I gave you the damn morphine. Now shut up before you get us both killed."

With that, he was finally quiet. I drew an M on his forehead with a black felt tip marker, indicating that a narcotic had been given, and began to drag him back to our side of the war. While I had been focused on my patient, Gonzales and another Marine had moved up to my position. According to Gonzales, they had spotted and shot a sniper, who was up in a tree, probably the guy who had shot Latane and who was going after me next. With the NVA machine gun and sniper out of commission, we were gaining momentum.

As I looked around the battlefield, I realized that Latane had slipped down over the steep side of the hill where only a mountain goat or Native American could stay upright and had crawled up behind the enemy soldiers in order to knock them out. Probably not a great plan, in retrospect, but it had worked. I hope he got a medal besides the Purple Heart for his actions. I would later initial a report citing his bravery.

Now with air and artillery fire covering us, we pulled back to safety. While our pilot's accuracy was usually good, you still wanted to be a respectful distance away when a five hundred pound bomb exploded. To evacuate the wounded and dead, we established an LZ a safe distance back. I found my two "bodyguards" and chewed them up one wall and down the other for leaving me alone out there.

It had been a grueling day so far, and now I had a whole new kind of problem. Another of the FNGs who had arrived just a few days earlier was apparently suffering from battle fatigue. He was doing the "Who am I-where are we-who are you" routine.

I was not completely sure that I believed him. Something just did not feel right to me, so I was keeping a close watch. He kept asking for water from everyone he saw. We had been on high ground long enough to be conserving water. His constant babble was beginning to irritate the seasoned troops and undermine the confidence of the replacements. It became annoying enough that, after an hour or so, the question was asked, "Doc, where can we shoot him that we won't kill him but will get him out of here?"

Right about that time, someone began passing out mail that had come in on one of the evacs. When they called out his name, he suddenly knew who he was again. He had been busted. I had been taught that in real battle fatigue the patient loses the ability to keep focus and becomes quiet and withdrawn. I told him that scared was okay because we were all scared, but he had a job to do, just like the rest of us. This may not seem very sympathetic, but I could not do my job if I was preoccupied with him. As we were still on the perimeter, I did the best thing I could do at the time. I turned him over to the BAS crew who were farther away from the perimeter. With them, he would not get himself killed by his own fear.

Late that evening and through the night, we listened to the voices of the NVA. They were usually very quiet and disciplined. Now, with as much noise as they were making, they sounded like a troop of Girl Scouts on a picnic. We could also hear the rumble of at least one tracked vehicle. This was very disconcerting, and while we did not want to believe it, most of us thought we would soon be facing off against tanks. These sounds, along with our own Phantoms and artillery shells, continued through the night. It was all very unnerving. Needless to say, sleep came in bits and pieces that night, if it came at all.

## ONCE MORE INTO THE BREECH

Daybreak and a hasty breakfast, and we headed out again. Yesterday's battleground had been pounded hard, but we still moved cautiously with Mike on point. At six feet four, Mike was one of the biggest guys in the platoon, and he usually had our platoon's unofficial mascot on his shoulder. This was an invisible white duck, which we just called White Duck. I think White Duck came from a bottle of Silver Fox whiskey mixed with a vivid imagination and silliness.

Dave Murray, second squad leader and my good friend, was second in line. A rifleman, the M-79 man, and I followed him. Then came Fitzgibbons and the others in his M-60 machine gun team. Fitz was our California surfer dude. He was never shy about laying down heavy fire and would carry extra barrels to replace those he had burned out. We were followed by the rest of the Second Platoon, First Platoon, and HQ, with the Third Platoon bringing up the rear.

The trail took us back across the saddle ridge that was the spot of the previous day's battle. About one hundred yards out, the path cut left. With the fourth man barely making the bend in the trail, we heard *Clack, clack, clack.*

All hell had broken loose again. I jumped behind a big tree, became as small as I could, and watched splinters of bark flying off both sides of the trunk around me. With a grenade in my right hand, I signaled to the Marines on both sides of me. They pulled out their grenades, pulled the pins, and got ready. I stood up, the bark still flying at about knee height. Holding up three fingers, I counted back three—two—one, and we all tossed our grenades in the direction I had pointed. I would like to think that we scared the dickens out of whoever was there and that they ran off. Whatever the case, the shooting stopped from that position, and just in time because I heard Dave shout, "Pig Pen! Get your ass up here."

Once again I was running, fast and low, into what I knew would be sure trouble with my logical brain telling me all the while to go the other way. As I turned the bend, I could see Dave about fifteen yards ahead looking for me. There was a six-inch tree trunk between him and the enemy. When he saw me, he half fell and half dived across the trail toward a foxhole on the opposite side. With his M-16 on full automatic, he covered my approach.

So I got to thinking as I covered that last ten yards that I might actually make it to that hole alive. I would get into the foxhole with Dave and be able to treat his wounds, and I was close to jumping in when I realized that both Mike and Dave were already inside. There was no room for me. I skidded to an ungraceful halt and ended up lying sideways against the enemy fire, with my head and chest in the hole, sort of, and my backside stretched across the trail.

"Treat Mike first," Dave said. "He's been hit the worst."

This may or may not have been true, but Dave would argue the point, and there was no time for debate. Mike's arm was broken; one medium battle dressing with strong pressure covered both the entrance and exit wounds. By leaving the ties long, I could temporarily splint the arm to his body. As I was doing this, dirt and rocks were stinging the left side of my face. The crack of the bullets was hurting my ears, and I was shouting for our M-60 team to cover us. When Mike was patched up, I went to work on Dave, who had in-and-out wounds on both an arm and a leg. The arm was broken but the leg was not; I applied a tight dressing on this calf and splinted his arm as I had Mike's. Dave told me about the enemy machine gun shooting at us. Even with all the pounding we had given them, the NVA had set in about twenty yards back from the previous day's position. This information did not make my legs or fanny feel too safe where they were. I tightened everything I had as close to the ground as I could. It's called the pucker factor. By the time Dave's arm was dressed, our M-60 and M-16 fire was much heavier than that of the enemy but not any higher above me. I became aware of Marines moving closer and finally pushing past me, as the First Platoon advanced through us to press the attack. Thankfully, I was no longer pinned down. I had another wounded man to treat, and Mike and Dave were safe where they were for the time being. The third man was beside the M-60 team.

"Good thing that was a dud, Doc," someone said.

That seemed like a strange thing to say right then, so I asked him, "What are you talking about?"

He explained that while I was head down in the fighting hole, patching up Dave and Mike, an NVA grenade, called a Chi Com, rolled up about three inches from my left leg but did not explode. Being as it was too late to be scared, I just took in a deep breath and said, "Yeah, a good thing."

We had to get our wounded together and get them to the LZ. The dust-off birds were in the air, and the remainder of Charlie Company was still advancing up the mountain in pursuit of the retreating NVA. Doc Paul and Doc Sieb had again come up and were now busy treating the wounded with me. I was glad because there were too many for me to handle alone.

In 2010, I would attended a 1/9 Battalion reunion, where I would listen to Dave's version of this incident. He insisted that I include his side of the story because I had obviously forgotten a few things. So here goes David's side of the story.

*Mike was on point, just ahead of me, and when the firing started, both of us were hit. Mike fell to the right side of the trail behind some trees, and I was knocked down to the left. My rifle had been knocked out of my hands. I could see the two NVA that had shot me and I was looking for my M-16. When I turned to my left, I saw both my hands and thought that my right arm had been shot off. With my left hand, I was able to reach my rifle. The NVA were standing up talking, and not knowing the language, I could not understand what they were saying. I got up to my knees, leveled my M-16, and shot both of them across their chests. I called for "Pig Pen," and with one hand was able to put another magazine in my rifle. I looked up, and here comes Doc John running up the trail. Doc had his 45 out and was blasting away. Kapow! Kapow! Kapow! Doc never missed a step or a shot. Reaching down, Doc's left hand grabbed my collar, and he dragged me to cover. I told Doc to patch Mike first. All the time Doc was working on us, he was also reloading my M-16 for me. Doc patched us up, tied the evacuation tags to our shirts, and ordered the guys to get us back to the landing zone. This is the way I remember the events of that day.*

I assigned a couple of troops to help the rest of the wounded back to the LZ and moved forward to catch up with the rest of our company. Our guys were now safely out of harm's way and being attended by Doctor Pasker and the BAS crew. They were awaiting dust-off, and the active fighting still needed corpsmen. Sergeant Brookshire had also been wounded in that firefight. Before leaving, he had asked me to look after his shotgun until he could get back. With the fighting this close in, I figured it might come in handy. Carrying the newly acquired twelve gauge, I moved past the spot of my earlier work and out of the trees.

For about thirty yards, I was walking through a field of eight- to ten-foot-high elephant grass. It ended abruptly, and I stepped out onto a very well-worn road. Looking to my right, I saw a burning half-track vehicle; beyond that, our Marines were moving tactically forward. Then I heard a sound, and I turned to face left. Eight feet away was the business end of an NVA artillery piece, the black hole of the barrel looking as big as a basketball and pointing directly at me. Pucker Factor! As I held my breath, my heart skipped a beat or two. I just knew this was the end. I began to compose "The Letter" in my head.

*"Dear Mr. and Mrs. Holm,*
*The President regrets to inform you that we are sending all the pieces of your son that we could find in this envelope . . ."*

But no explosion occurred. The sound that I did hear, a strange moaning, was coming not from NVA preparing to shoot but instead from a couple of wounded Marines. I ran to them.

They had used the heavy armor plating of the big gun for cover as they advanced. They were behind it when an RPG round had blown up against it. The steel plate had saved them from shrapnel, but both were suffering from concussions, ruptured eardrums, and scrambled thought processors. I thought they would be all right if there were no major internal injuries. I assigned a couple of Marines to get them back to the LZ and moved back up the road. I passed the bombed out half-track. This was the "tank" I had heard last night. It had been used to pull the big guns. I was relieved that it was not an actual tank.

I treated the wounded as I came to them, returning a favor by helping an overloaded fellow corpsman. I sent the wounded back to the LZ, in groups of two or three, with an escort. It was apparent that our aggressive attack was working. The enemy was retreating right into our air and artillery strikes, and into the arms of a bunch of Marines who were dug in and waiting for them.

That night, we made camp on top of the mountain. Just inside our lines lay the body of a dead NVA soldier who had been lethally burned by napalm. Sergeant Christensen said, "Leave him so for the troops to see."

I did just that for an hour or so, but after I had dug my foxhole for the night, I went back and covered him with an abandoned poncho and then buried him. I used the excuse that he was a health hazard to our guys and would start to smell very bad very soon. I pounded a good-sized stick in the ground above his head and hung his pith hat on it to mark the site so that his comrades could find him, if they did that sort of thing. I know that we made every possible effort to leave no man behind on the field of battle. Just for the record, I never witnessed any collecting or displaying of ears or other body parts by the men with whom I served. We were warriors and had a certain respect for other warriors, which included the NVA.

We continued to push up the valley into an area called the Parrot's Beak. On the map, the border with Laos resembled the head and beak of a parrot. According to the map, the border was seventy yards to our left, near the tree line. We were moving in combat spread across a fairly open area of waist-high grass. There was a distance of about ten yards between each man. I was thinking how we had been hit every day now for at least the last two weeks, when the *whoosh* of RPGs and *clack, clack* of AK-47s from the tree line disrupted the silence. I dove into a nearby bomb crater, already occupied by three Marines. A thin row of five-feet-tall brush growing along one section of the rim separated us from the incoming fire. I immediately went to work on an arm wound. Tucking ourselves against the side of the crater nearest the enemy gave us the most protection. The volume of the incoming bullets created a shower of leaves and small branches falling all around us. I bandaged the wound on the Marine's arm and heard another call. I moved to the edge of the crater and saw our radioman, sitting out in the open, approximately twenty yards away. There was a look of shock on his face. The stalks of grass were falling steadily between us, as if some invisible scythe were sweeping through the field.

"Gomer. Get down!" I shouted.

I motioned for him to crawl over to the relative safety of the crater. He got to his hands and knees and, to my horror, a thin red line appeared across his forehead. Blood began to flow down into his eyes. My mind was racing. I had promised my mother and girlfriend that I would not do anything stupid, and what I was contemplating was downright insane. I had a man down, with only one way to get to him, and that was straight through a hail of fire. I could think of no way to cross that distance without getting hit.

The next thing I remember is sliding back down the side of that crater and pulling him in with me. To this day, I honestly do not remember going out there to get him, but I do know he was in no shape to have come to me. He had been shot through the right hand and arm, and a third round had channeled a groove, three to four inches long and a half-inch wide, across his forehead and skull. The hand and arm wounds were easy enough to treat, but the head wound dressing had to be snug enough to stop the bleeding but not so tight as to squeeze the cerebral tissue from the wound. The bullet had already destroyed some brain tissue, and I did not want him to lose any more. By now, we were fully engaged with the enemy. The wounded that could were returning fire, and I could hear Lieutenant Webster moving toward our position and giving directions to the men along the way.

I treated the wounds that I knew of and again crawled over to the edge of the crater to alert Lieutenant Webster of our position. He was crouched and running fast toward us, when suddenly he jerked to the right and went down hard.

"LT! Are you hit?" I called out.

"I don't think so. Stay put. I'm coming to you," he replied.

When he finally slid into the crater, he started to direct the men. I did a quick exam that revealed no wounds. I glanced over and noticed a Marine who was trying to "help me" by tightening the battle dressing on the head of our radioman. I directed my attention back to preserving the radioman's grade school education by not squeezing his gray matter out of the wound. By the time I looked back, Lieutenant Webster was on his way up the line, moving swiftly from man to man, directing fire and looking for a working radio. The bullet that had hit the RTO's hand had also destroyed the talking part of the handset.

We continued the firefight, and somebody with a working radio called in air support. When the Phantoms arrived, we kept our heads down to avoid the rocks and scrap metal now flying overhead as a result of the close air support. The air strikes quickly turned the momentum of the fight in our favor, and the battle finally ended. With no more wounded and everyone stable at this site, I took two smoke grenades from the wounded radioman. I went to look for additional wounded, our second radio (being carried by a brand new radio operator), and a usable spot for an LZ. We had a dust-off bird inbound. I located the backup handset with the new RTO, and an LZ site at about the same time. Discarding the broken handset and replacing it with the working one, I sent a runner to start moving the wounded to the LZ. I got on the medical evacuation frequency and started talking to the inbound helicopters, instructing the new man on this procedure. I had learned this from the wounded RTO. Luckily for him, I was a good student. In about thirty minutes, the wounded were on their way to the care of highly skilled Navy doctors on the *USS Repose*. Evacuation had taken a little longer than usual because we were so far inland.

We reorganized and went after the enemy again but made no further contact. Later, as we sat down to grab a bite to eat, I was sitting near Lieutenant Webster and discovered why he had gone down so hard earlier.

"Those dirty little SOBs shot me in my Beanie Weenies," he said.

He opened his pack and pulled an olive green C-ration can with a hole on each side. Light brown juice dripped down the side of the can with the occasional brown bean. The bullet also put sixteen holes in his rolled up sweatshirt and shattered his bottle of Texas Pete Tabasco Sauce, which he had gotten in a care package from home. He had wrapped the Texas Pete in his sweatshirt to protect it from breakage.

I have been in touch with Lieutenant Webster since and asked him if he recalled that incident. He certainly did, and he tells me he still has that sweatshirt.

# HO CHI MINH MART

The battalion column was again on the move along the main branch of the Ho Chi Minh trail. It was an improved, hard-packed road along this section. We were in an area of forest beneath a thick overhead canopy when we made an amazing discovery. In a hand-dug cave along one side of the road were more than fifty steel barrels of gasoline and a large number of empties. Further up the road were many other such bunkers filled with food, uniforms, mortar tubes and rounds, rifles still packed in cosmolene (a light grease) and then wrapped in brownish-yellow, water-resistant paper. There were radios, mess kits, backpacks, a bicycle repair shop with all kinds of spare parts, and a large parking area with several howitzer-type artillery pieces. We found hundreds, if not thousands, of boxes of bullets for rifles and pistols, and shells for the big guns. In short, everything an army needed to stay in the field and fight a war. It was no wonder we were seeing so much enemy resistance. They were trying to protect this stuff. The top brass were like kids on Christmas morning. We had scored big and had pushed so hard that the NVA had left this supply complex without even disabling the weapons.

Charlie Company and some of the HQ Company were left behind to protect, inventory, and destroy the weapons. A landing zone was cleared, and the food was lifted out and given to the people in the refuge camps. Flying Cranes and Chinooks hoisted out the big guns. They would end up at various military bases, museums, and on the front lawns of county courthouses across America. The engineers were placing explosive charges in the fuel dump and other supply bunkers. Any stuff lying around loose was being placed in bomb craters where it would later be blown up. I took one of the SKS rifles as a war souvenir, as did several other men.

Several of my friends and I were sitting down having lunch and talking. We were aware of the activity around us, but for a few minutes we were taking a rest from hauling things around. About one hundred yards down the hill, one of the craters was being filled with small arms ammunition and mortar rounds. Three men were working there when, suddenly, there was an explosion, followed by an immediate fire within the crater. I could see that two of the Marines working there were down and not moving. Dropping my lunch, I grabbed my satchel of dressings and headed downhill. As I got closer, the pistol and/or rifle ammo began to "cook off" from the fire. The inside of the crater, as well as the air around it, was fast becoming a very unhealthy place to be. Pieces of hot scrap metal, dirt, rocks, and wood splinters from the ammo crates were being blasted out of the pit. The inside of this crater was already a pretty inhospitable place, so using the small brim of dirt at the edge for cover, I stuck an arm in, grabbed a handful of uniform and dragged the first man out. Fortunately, there was a lull in the explosions, which I hoped would last. I went in for the second one. My friends were not far behind, and with their help, we managed to drag the injured men behind some big rocks, where I could treat their wounds. The injuries were serious enough but not life-threatening. I knew they were going to be all right. We carried them to the LZ where they were soon picked up.

Since our main RTO had been seriously wounded, and the second radio was being carried by a man new to the job, I now had an additional duty. I had spent a lot of my time with the platoon command post and have always had an insatiable appetite for learning, so it turned out that the most experienced RTO we had was me. I found myself now carrying an extra twenty or so pounds of radio and batteries, enough to convince me I did not want that job. Throw into the equation the fact that the two jobs often took me in opposite directions, and that the corpsman, RTO, and lieutenant were the top three targets the NVA wanted to hit. I now occupied two of those positions. With a couple of days assigned to provide security for the final cleanup, Lieutenant Webster assigned another man to the RTO spot. Almost all Marines have some radio training, so in a relatively short amount of time, the new RTO had the basics and was able to do his job well enough that he only needed the lieutenant or me for an occasional question.

Not wanting to let up the pressure on the retreating enemy, we extracted what we could in two days, and the rest was blown up. We began humping fairly hard to catch up with the rest of the battalion. Some replacements had joined us while we had been there, and the one that I was most happy to meet was a Navy corpsman. I do not remember if Stewart was his first or last name, but he was quickly dubbed Doc Stu. I introduced him around to the troops and started to help him break in. It was a fast pace for those of us who were used to it, so I am sure the only thing the new men had going for them was the fact that they were a bit more rested. We were all tired and would not catch the main body that night, but we found a good spot to set in and make camp.

This had to be a rough day for our new guys, but knowing we would not be up with the rest of the battalion by nightfall was a relief. We would be providing a protective element to their rear, and we could actually stop a bit earlier in the day so as to gain a bit more rest. Gene, Doc Stu, and I found an abandoned bunker in great shape in which to spend the night. After checking it out for occupants and booby traps, we moved in. It was constructed of eight- to ten-inch logs, placed in an A-frame design that was buried at the peak, at least six feet below the ground. I could stand up straight in the center, and there was plenty of floor space. Entry was through a narrow ditch, and I believed it could withstand some serious air or artillery strikes. Since a good amount of daylight remained, I set up a sick call.

We had several cases of jungle rot because of the constant rain. The men came over, one at a time, so I could treat their legs and feet. Our water had to be kept for drinking purposes, so washing off was not high on anyone's to-do list. I was using some of my drinking water supply and the captured soap to clean the wounds. I knew my own well-being depended on the men being in the best shape possible. My makeshift office was set up at the edge of our bunker entry. After about an hour, I had seen and treated everyone. I put my supplies back in my pack, took it down into the bunker, and came back out to relax and discuss our daily routine with Doc Stu.

Three or four minutes into our conversation, my internal alarm system went off, and I quickly dropped into our trenched entrance, pulling Stu by the shirt as I went for the ground. The *whoosh* of the RPG round passing through the airspace where I had just been sitting and the *boom* of the explosion triggered a response in me I had not really felt before. For the first time in eight months, instead of the usual measured cautiousness and fear, I was now feeling an intense anger. Until now the enemy had been, for the most part, shooting at bushes, trees, and rocks that I was using as cover, and somehow, I had accepted that situation as being a part of combat and had never taken it personally. The rulebook, the Geneva Convention, forbids targeting medics. The shooter would have seen me treating the Marines and known that I was a medic. He had fired from a clump of brush that was surrounded by very little cover so he had to have been hiding there for some time. I had been the specific target. Inside the bunker, I was seething with rage. I had to shoot back, but the only weapons available to me were three 45 caliber pistols and two shotguns. None had the necessary range to cover the distance to the puff of smoke now rising above where he had fired. I grabbed my medical bag and headed topside. I had to see if anyone had been hurt, and I wanted to find a rifle. Knowing there was basically no cover until I cleared the top of the hill twenty yards away, I popped out of my entry trench at a full run. On the sheltered side of the hill, I skidded to a halt and found that nobody had been injured. I grabbed a loaded M-16 and moved to the crest of the hill. For a long time, I stood there, firing into that small clump of bushes. This guy had shot at me, in spite of the fact that I was a medic. I had honored the warrior's code and expected the same from others. His action had been a personal affront. After laying a heavy volume of fire into the opposite hillside, and by now six other Marines had joined me in shooting, we received no more incoming fire.

By now, I had reconciled myself to the fact that most of the incoming fire was addressed "To Whom It May Concern," but this guy had pissed me off. I had learned another thing about myself that day. That there are dark places inside me of which I am not overly proud. Places that will and must be forever in the past.

## CLOSING THE TRAP

We caught up with the main part of our unit on a mountain called Tam Boi. We were now at the point that essentially closed the backdoor on the enemy retreat. They were now between the hammer and the anvil, being pounded both from the air and the artillery now surrounding them. Their only escape routes would lead them through the fresher units positioned in front or the snarling angry dog that had been nipping at their heels for the past month. That was us. To say we were platoon-sized patrols, at this point, was a misnomer. Due to our losses, we were now squad-sized patrols. At least twice a day, these patrols came at them from both sides (the hammer and the anvil), keeping them pinned between us.

On one such patrol, we made our way along the side of a valley created by two finger-like ridges. An NVA patrol, of similar size, was doing the same on the opposite side. When we spotted each other, they turned and hurried back the way they had come, without a shot being fired. *It was not a good day to die,* I guess. Our forward observer (FO) called in a fire mission in their direction of retreat.

The next day, an Alpha Company patrol discovered more bunkers and more supplies. Soon, firefights became a daily routine. We went out again and made brief contact after moving only about four hundred yards beyond our lines. I do not think that this was a planned ambush as much as it was their patrol accidentally running into ours. I hustled up to the side of a wounded man. It was the same guy who had been unable to remember his name until mail call. A bullet hole in his helmet, right where his forehead would be, with an exit hole in the back, a mere inch up from the edge, diminished any hope for him.

Suddenly, bullets began to impact around us. They were coming from behind. The only areas of cover were two separate stands of small trees and a clump of brush. Grabbing the wounded man's rifle, I asked the lieutenant and radioman to shoot into one clump of trees. The machine gunner worked the brushy area. The remaining stand of trees was mine. After we were done shooting, we were no longer being shot at from behind at least, and I turned my attention back to my patient. I still call this man the Luckiest Marine Alive. I was amazed to discover that his helmet's liner deflected the bullet, which then tumbled between the one-sixteenth-inch fiberglass layer and the steel on the outside before exiting out the back. It had torn up the liner and created a linear laceration straight from front to back along his scalp. By some miracle, his wound was only skin deep. While Marines are not known for having long hair, we had been out in the field for some weeks, and his hair had grown long enough for my purposes. I had run out of packaged suture material. Improvising, I used strands of his hair along the edges of the wound as sutures to close the wound. This would work very well until he could get to the doctors in the rear, who would shave his head in order to treat the wound properly. It would also save them the trouble of locating and removing temporary stitches. By the time I had completed the wound closure and applied a dressing, more men had come up from camp to reinforce us. I had him moved back to the LZ for evacuation. I still wonder if the folks at the hospital end marveled at my creativity or just thought I was crazy.

An hour or so later, I had, for the second time in a week, another close encounter with an RPG. It *whooshed* over my head, smacked into a tree directly behind me, and exploded on impact. I was not injured, but the concussion gave me a serious headache. It was the kind of headache where you can hear your hair growing, and it lasted well into the next day. After repeated contact throughout the day, we stayed out on ambush that entire night.

The next day, we returned to our main encampment to discover that they had come under mortar fire through the night. My friend Gene was very upset; it seems his air mattress had been a "casualty of war" after having sustained multiple shrapnel wounds. I declared it killed in action. He had carried that extra three pounds of weight a long way and had blown it up every night so that he could sleep comfortably. He had more than a few unkind words for the NVA soldier who had fired that mortar round.

"That no good slant-eyed little . . ." Let me just say he went on and on about the man and his parentage. He also offered up several suggestions of things the NVA soldier might do to himself. Many of them, I am fairly certain, are physically impossible. I should point out that a combat soldier's vocabulary, even with the use of very short words, could be exceptionally colorful. After he had blown off a little steam, I placed my hand on his shoulder and said, "I'm glad you weren't on it when it got killed."

This had been a long operation. It was a challenge both physically and emotionally.

About now, in this operation, I became very concerned that I could be killed or captured. Fatigue, hunger, and stress were putting a few dents in the armor of my feeling nine feet tall and bulletproof. Mortars, RPGs, and rifles had shot at us every single day now for over a month. I had already survived several months beyond the average life expectancy for a combat corpsman. If we were overrun, I did not want my stateside addresses or the personal pictures I had carried of family and friends to fall into enemy hands. With so much sadness, I took a long last look at each one and made a small bonfire. To this fire, I also committed my journal. Even now, the memory of that day saddens me. So much was written on those pages that would have made the telling of these stories much easier.

We had been on the high ground for several days now, and the frequent fighting, constant moving, and monsoon rains had made receiving supplies very difficult. Attempts were made to parachute some supplies in to us, but most landed outside our lines or wound up in the tops of trees. No way that we could retrieve them without starting a firefight. For three days, we had no breakfast. Lunch consisted of a canteen cup filled with hot water and a package of dehydrated bouillon from one of the care packages I had received from home. For a bit of body, I harvested grass seeds and tender leaves from tips of bushes and added them. It was shared among ten to twelve men. The first couple of days, supper was the same cup with a packet of Kool-Aid. The next couple of days, we had some Sucral diet-sweetener tablets. The thinking was that we might fool our bodies into the belief they were getting some actual sugar. When the sweetener was gone, we just had water. At least water was plentiful, as we were soaking wet all the time. But drinking water was in short supply. If we sent a patrol down to the river, they would be ambushed. I did not even worry about wearing my poncho. I just set it up to shelter my gear and catch rainwater. With some creative construction, rainwater and the dew that settled at night dripped into well-placed canteens. My seventh canteen was always topped off first and was still used only for the wounded.

While not on radio watch, Doc Stu and I slept about ten feet behind the perimeter, under the shelter constructed from our ponchos. The size of the platoon had become so small that we could only man half a dozen holes; we were close to all our troops. Now we stood radio watch in a fighting hole on the line. We took incoming rounds both day and night, as the NVA tried to find a weak spot to break out of their trap. They had fresh troops coming in behind us from their bases in Laos. One rainy night, around 2:00 a.m., we again started taking incoming mortar rounds. I shook Doc Stu on his shoulder, "Get to the foxhole!"

He rolled out, slid down the incline, and *sploosh* he was in our fighting hole, which now had six inches of water in the bottom. So I got to thinking as I pulled my flak jacket tight around me, pushed my helmet down on my head, and muttered, "If they haven't been able to kill me in this amount of time, the little bastards aren't going to get me tonight."

I hated wet feet to the extent that I had been known to sit down in the middle of a combat patrol and change into dry socks, a particular practice that drove Sergeant Christensen crazy. The next round hit approximately six feet away, and before the sparks had all settled, *sploosh*, my feet were wet.

"Damn it," I said to no one.

Dawn came slowly, and we found ourselves even more wet, cold, tired, hungry, and not quite sure of our future. We were receiving a steady barrage of incoming mortar fire, and our lines were being hit at several locations by rifle fire. While this was causing the NVA to deplete their supplies further, I still would have preferred taking it away from them and blowing it up.

A few days before, we had been joined by a company of Army Special Forces, who had been working to our west. The Marine forces on the surrounding ridges had also sent in a couple of platoon-sized patrols. The added numbers helped. Even so, we were slowly pulling the line in around our LZ.

We had been out of food for three days now; even my bouillon was gone, and we were also running low on ammunition. The weather had cleared some but it was still very overcast, and if we did not get some transportation soon, I feared we might run out of time. Trees had been cut or blown down, and trenches had been dug in the LZ to shelter the men who would be huddled in groups awaiting the helicopters. *If only we could get them in*, I thought. If we couldn't, the trenches would be the sites of our last stand. We did have some air support with the O-1 Birddogs overhead. They were spotting for the Phantoms and the Helicopter Gunships, both Cobras and Hueys, now circling our position. We were often down in our fighting holes being showered by dirt and debris, as our air cover was working very close in to be effective. It helped to slow the NVA down but was not stopping them. A flight of Sea Knights showed up. They made a pass, and our sprits soared until we watched them pulling away. They claimed the zone was too hot to land. At times, we were able to see the advancing enemy. I was busy with the frequent bandaging of wounds and keeping the injured men within the shrinking perimeter. My thoughts drifted back a few days to the last med-evac that had come in. I could see the inbound helicopter in the distance. Having no time to write a letter, I had addressed an envelope and written in the space under the flap.

Dear Mom and Dad,

I'm OK.

Love, John.

I gave the flap a quick lick, and when the Huey touched down, I ran up and handed my "letter" to the door gunner. He slipped it into his shirt pocket and gave me a thumbs-up.

Across the valley, a flight of four Army Chinooks from the 101st Air Wing, the Black Cats, appeared; they turned and headed toward us. We rejoiced when they managed to set down, two at a time, in our LZ. We were now taking a good amount of combined mortar and small arms fire. My hat is off, once again, to the courage and bravery of these pilots, even more so since our own Marine flyers had whimped out on us. After the first two were loaded and again airborne, we took our place in one of the trenches, firing with all we had left. As the second set of Chinooks set down, I picked up one of our wounded and half ran, half stumbled up the ramp. With all of us aboard, we were soon airborne and on our way back to VCB.

I don't know the numbers for Charlie Company, but the way I remember it, of the original members of the Second Platoon and its reinforcements, we were now only twelve. A patient that I met recently, who himself was a former Marine, tells me that he had seen casualty reports that indicated only twelve men were left, unwounded, out of the whole of Charlie Company. No matter what the number, I was just glad to be among the upright.

As we flew back toward Vandergrift, my fondest wish was to sit down with a big block of ice in a bowl, and as the last bit melted, to drink the whole bowl of water and relish the absence of thirst. I settled for a stop at the water bull that was parked alongside the landing strip, where I filled my canteens. I downed two immediately.

It was on this operation I had discovered that banana trees are somewhat like cacti. If you cut a softball-sized piece from the trunk and sucked hard, it would yield about an ounce of slightly bitter-tasting liquid. When canteens were empty, any way to get fluids in was important. For over two months, I had carried around a beer, a leftover from New Year's, in the bottom of my pack. One of those nights, six of us split it. I hope that will forever be the only time in my life when I will say two ounces of warm beer really hits the spot.

Back at the company area, we had a very pleasant surprise. Several of the wounded from earlier were recovered and waiting to welcome us. It was great to see them and know that they were well. I usually did not know what happened to a wounded man once I placed him on the helicopter.

The official Marine reports on the operation are now declassified, and they state that we sustained 130 killed in action, 932 wounded in action, and one missing in action, while the North Vietnamese lost 1,617 killed in action. These were the ones we were able to see. We have no way of knowing the number of wounded, but the ratio of wounded to killed was usually considered to be about ten to one. We captured five prisoners. In all, we captured or destroyed 1,273 individual weapons, rifles, pistols, and RPG launchers, with 607,000 rounds of ammunition and 14,800 RPGs, sixteen artillery guns with 8,000 shells, ninety anti-aircraft guns with 145,00 rounds, eighty machine guns, 74,000 grenades and rockets, 3,000 mines, and twenty mortars with 62,000 rounds. That was real close to a million rounds of ammunition that would not be fired at anybody, and that's not even counting the number of rounds used up fighting with us. We also captured 126 bicycles, with many spare parts, as well as the repair shop, along with ninety-two motorized vehicles, with tools used in their repair, and 2,750 gallons of diesel fuel.

It was now March 1969, and we had prevented a repeat of the Tet Offensive that had occurred in 1968. Last, but certainly not the least, was 115 tons of food, including some live chickens, pigs, and a water buffalo, all of which went to the refugee camps. In retrospect, I wish we had held back a little for the few days we were out of chow. While we had been hit hard, we had definitely given back much more than we had taken. The battalion was awarded the Presidential Unit Citation for our actions.

## OUT OF THE BUSH

I received word from the battalion surgeon that Doc Stu would be taking over my assignment with the Second Platoon. I was to be assigned to the Battalion Aid Station at Vandergrift Combat Base for the rest of my tour. It was a bittersweet feeling for me. I had become so protective of the men who had been in my care for the past nine months that it was difficult to think of them going out into harm's way without me along. Word also was passed that the battalion was to go on an in-country rest and recreation that afternoon. So I walked over to BAS and talked my way into staying with the platoon until after the R&R.

While I had been up to BAS and/or walking along the right side of the parked convoy that was going to take us to Dong Ha, a childhood friend and neighbor named Dennis Coney had been walking along the left side. He had been talking to the men on the trucks trying to find me. We had grown up just a couple of blocks from each other and, from kindergarten through high school, had been friends. Half a world away from home and only separated by the width of a road. It would have been nice but was not meant to be. He later wrote home to his parents that he had tried to find me but was not able to. I did not become aware of his efforts until long after I got home.

We were soon all aboard the trucks and headed down Highway 9 to Dong Ha where we boarded an LST. The letters stood for Landing Ship Troops, and the ship resembled a very large beach landing craft with a flat front end, which dropped down to create a ramp for offloading men and vehicles. This was the first time in my Navy career that I was actually on a floating form of transportation. I was feeling quite good about the three-hour ride down to the South China Sea until I discovered that the sailors referred to the LST as a Large Slow Target.

Thankfully, the trip was smooth and without incident. For the next four days, we were able to eat real cooked meals, have a few beers, play cards, read books from the library, and listen to our music as loud as we wanted. We also had movies, a USO show—not Bob Hope—and a swim in the ocean. Ever the corpsman, I soon discovered that going barefoot and wading in the salt water did a wonderful job of clearing up jungle rot, so I made sure all the men were getting in the water a couple of times daily. This proved to be one of my easier and more enjoyable treatments both for myself and the Marines in my unit.

Hobo, and his handler Ron, both recovering nicely from their wounds, had rejoined us. I found my furry buddy in the bottom of a three-foot deep hole he had dug in the sand. He had a boony hat strapped on his head and was sleeping off a hangover in the cool damp sand. He had also had a couple of beers.

Another thing I learned while watching the local fisherman going out on the river for their daily catch was that military men, in their indomitable fashion, had even come up with a designation for these small bamboo-reed fishing boats. They called them LBGBs or Little Bitty Gook Boats. All in all, it was a great few days with the only reminder of the war being occasional gunfire a couple of miles up the beach, where there was a perimeter around us. There were also overflights by the Phantoms going to or from their carriers, and a few security helicopters.

We returned from R&R, and I moved to BAS. It was nearing the end of March, and I felt like I could officially consider myself a "short-timer." I only had until the end of May before I was to come off active duty. Even if they made me stay a full tour, until July 1, I figured it was down to less than a hundred days. Two-digit territory. Since I would not have to be loading everything I needed on my back every day, I was planning to go back to Quang Tri soon and pick up some clothes and personal items that would make my life more comfortable.

I was sitting on my cot writing a letter home. It was March 28, 1969. One of the corpsmen I had just met came into our tent and said, "Hey, are you John Holm?"

"Yes."

"Well, pack up your gear, man. You're going home. Your flight date is April 1."

"That's not even a funny April Fool's joke," I said, not believing it at first.

"Hey, man. They're your orders. If you don't want them, I'll take the flight."

After confirming my serial number, it sank in that I was a true "short-timer" with only three days and a wake-up left in country. These were the words that every man in country longed to hear, and I was thrilled, excited, overjoyed, ecstatic. I had made it! I was going home.

# IV

## BACK TO THE WORLD

Now, I had a lot to do and very little time to do it in. The first thing I did was to go down to the platoon area and say farewell to my buddies. Some of them had been assigned to security for the daily "minesweep," so I found myself walking down Highway 9, shaking hands, and saying good-bye. Murry McCann was on point, out in front of a tank, but behind the man with the minesweeper.

"Little Mac, hold up!" I shouted.

"Doc, you crazy squid! What are you doing walking point for a tank?"

"I'm going back to the world, Mac, two days and a wake-up."

"You lucky dog, Doc. Now get your ass back inside camp. This is no place for a short-timer."

I got back inside base camp and caught a ride with a convoy down Highway 9 to Dong Ha. I needed to fill out the necessary forms to register my SKS rifle with the FBI and Military Police and obtain a temporary importer's license so I could take it home. That accomplished, I caught a late afternoon ride north up Highway 1 to Quang Tri. Sticking out my thumb was still the easiest way to get from point A to point B and quite a bit less frightening than my first ride up this road.

I thought about that nervous young kid with shiny black boots who had stood beside this road last July so frightened and so naive. That seemed a lifetime ago. Was there anything left of him? I wondered if I would ever be able to fit back into a life of peace.

Fortunately, I did not have too long to ponder these questions before two cooks in a jeep stopped for me. They were retuning to Quang Tri after picking up some supplies, and I was sharing the back seat with a rather large slab of frozen hog destined for the officers' mess, no doubt. As we left the base, I slammed a full clip of rounds in my 45 and asked if they intended to lock and load the M-60 mounted on a post in back of the jeep. That is when I discovered that neither of them actually knew how to use it. Staying with the machine gun team had paid off once again. I felt a lot more comfortable once it was actually functional. I think it scared them a little since I had mentioned I was a displaced sailor, but I was too close to going home to be running around the countryside with no bullets. So I loaded the machine gun. It was late in the afternoon when we arrived at Quang Tri, so I said my thanks and good-byes to the army cooks. I found an evening meal and an empty cot and called it a day.

"Goooooooooood morning, Vietnam!"

It was the next to the last time I awoke to the familiar opening phrase of the new day. I made my way to the latrine and then to breakfast, for once looking forward to what the day would bring. My first stop was the Headquarters tent to pick up a checkout sheet, and then to all the other tents that I had passed through on the way in. I went to the Armory to turn in my 45, to Medical to obtain my health records, to Storage for my seabag, etc. With all my Ts crossed and Is dotted, I was back to Headquarters to pick up my orders and then down to the LZ to catch a Sea Knight on to Dong Ha. No more road trips in this country for me. The airport was more secure now than it had been nine months earlier, but still as rustic. Soon, I was on a cargo plane headed for Da Nang.

The tent motel for arriving and departing troops was still there, so I found an empty cot and stowed my gear under it. Then I found the mess hall. That night, I watched the arriving young men, wide-eyed and fearful, all wearing shining black boots. I could not help but wonder how many of them would get to pass back through in a year. I tucked my dirty scuffed-up boots under my cot and dropped off to sleep.

"Gooooooooooooood morning, Vietnam."

It was April 1. For the last time in country, I endured bag inspection. All my paperwork was checked again. The last of my combat gear was turned in. Before too long, my "freedom bird" taxied up on the tarmac. All of us who boarded were still anxious. I felt a whole lot better when that shiny plane's body angled toward the sky, the landing gear thumped into the up and closed position, and the view out of the window was the coastline of Vietnam receding behind us. My mind was filled with the elation of having survived the past nine months and once again feeling safe, but I could not stop the unanswered questions that were also creeping in. Are my friends at VCB or out in the bush? Are they receiving their malaria pills? Do they need me? I didn't want to leave my friends, but I wanted to leave Vietnam.

It was a short hop up to Okinawa, where we received health checks and endured more paper pushing. In all, I spent about a week there standing in various lines. I alternated worrying about my buddies and thinking "Just let me go home."

On April 8, I was boarding a very large Intercontinental 707, with a hundred or so equally happy GIs, on my way back to The World. The World meant any place other than where we had been.

For most of us, the flight attendants were the first round-eyed women we had seen in a long time. It was probably prime duty for them, knowing there would be no unhappy passengers on these flights, but I still say these were brave women. It was about 1600 hours (4:00 p.m.) Saturday afternoon, local time, as the sleek silver nose of the airplane lifted off the runway and pointed east.

The initial flight plan called for us to make a stop in Hawaii to take on fuel, but the weather there had turned really bad, so the pilot announced we would be going straight on to San Francisco. Both he and the flight crew assured us that we had enough fuel to make it nonstop. During the flight, we again crossed the International Dateline, so when we landed in California, it was 8:00 a.m. on the same date we had taken off. After flying fourteen hours, we landed about eight hours before we took off, and I do not think I slept at all. To look out of the window and see the California coast was wonderful. No longer would I have to sleep with snakes and bugs. No longer would going for food and water be a life-threatening trip. No longer would I have to sleep at night with a loaded pistol under my head. I was back in The World. I was finally safe.

There were several buses waiting for us on the tarmac. I do not know where the Army and Air Force guys went, but the Marine and Navy men were taken to Treasure Island, where we were assigned to a barrack and our orders were processed once more. We were designated as casual company. This was an ever-changing group of men coming through while orders were being processed. Some stayed a day or two and moved on, but since I was coming off active duty, I would be spending about a week. The first thing I did, after finding a bunk and locker, was to head down to the payphones at the "Gee Dunk." This was an on-base version of a mini mart. While waiting for a phone, I bought my first candy bar in nine months that was not packaged in a tin can. The refined sugar was so sweet! I took two bites and sat down as it went straight to my head. I called both Three Rivers and Detroit. Having assured everyone that I was back in the US of A and that I was safe, I went back to the barrack, crawled into my bunk, and slept for the next sixteen hours.

Those days were filled with hurry-up-and-wait processing lines, eating meals, picking up litter, and keeping the barracks clean. When we had completed what we had to do each day, we were granted liberty. I would usually read a book and try to pass the time on base. I knew that Vietnam veterans were not getting a warm and fuzzy welcome-home reception at that time. But that didn't matter to me because I was going home.

One day, I decided that since I was in San Francisco, which was home of the infamous topless bars, I needed to see one, at least once. Dressed in civilian clothes, I took a bus to town and found a topless bar. It did not take long before I figured out that once was enough. I had not seen an American woman in over nine months, but these dancers were very plain and either bored or annoyed, I couldn't tell which. Most of the customers in the bar just ignored them. I felt sorry for these women. Being totally underwhelmed, I finished my overpriced drink and went back to base, my curiosity satisfied.

Finally, the day came when all the paperwork was completed and I headed for the airport for my flight to Detroit. I purchased a standby ticket expecting to be on the red-eye. It was early yet, and a seat became available on a late afternoon flight, so I took it. I arrived at Detroit Metro Airport around midnight. Harriet was already at work, expecting to pick me up after her eleven-to-seven shift. By this time, I was used to waiting for things to fall in place. Since she was the first person I wanted to see, I would just sit tight until she got there.

I was in the North Terminal, which was practically deserted at that hour, so I went up to the second level and found a couch-like row of seats. Placing the SKS rifle between the wall and myself, I stretched out and went to sleep. Before long, an airport security officer came by and informed me that I was loitering and could not sleep there. I asked if sitting in a chair would be acceptable, and he said that it would be. Okay. Go figure. Asleep sitting in a chair is not loitering, but lying down is. *It must have something to do with comfort*, I thought. He moved on, and I got up, put on my shoes, and moved back down to the main floor. I was in my Navy dress blue uniform and was carrying the rifle out in the open so that it could not be considered a concealed weapon. I found a standard airport plastic chair with metal legs and sat down. I placed my left arm and leg through the strap of one seabag. I put my AWOL bag under my chair, and my right arm and leg went through the strap of the second seabag and sling of the SKS that had the bolt removed. I again fell asleep. Suddenly, the sixth sense that had saved my life more than once during the past year went off in my head. I very slowly opened my eyes to discover about twelve airport police officers fanned out in a semi-circle across the main floor of the terminal, advancing toward me. This was long before the days of terrorists hijacking airplanes, and I really did not think much about having the rifle. After all, I had been armed every day for quite a while. As my eyes opened fully, they stopped, and each one put a hand on his sidearm.

"Can I help you, gentlemen?"

"We need to see the gun," one of them said.

"It is a rifle, not a gun, and as you can see, it has the bolt removed, empty chamber exposed. If we can all relax a bit, I will be glad to show it to everybody."

I slowly took my leg out of the sling, and holding the barrel, raised it off the floor, stock out. As one of the officers took possession of my rifle, I told them, "I am now going to reach into my pocket, very slowly, for papers only."

I pulled out the FBI and Military Police registration forms, along with the import license. I explained what they were and stated, "I will take my rifle back now, if you please."

Apparently, no one had enough authority to make a decision, so they ushered me off to the County Police Substation, about a mile away, to confer with their duty lieutenant. Just to needle them a little, I asked them to tote my seabags to the car while I carried my AWOL bag and my orders. It was kind of funny to see each seabag carrier huffing and puffing as they carried less than half of what I had been hauling around. After driving me down to their station, they left me in a chair out front while they went into the office to talk with their duty officer. Knowing I could not be in a much safer spot than a police station, I once again closed my eyes and took a nap.

After hearing the stories his men had to tell, the lieutenant came out to talk to me.

"Just getting home from Nam, son?"

"Yes, sir."

"What can you tell me about this rifle?"

"A war souvenir, sir. It's a Chinese-made SKS, 7.64 millimeter, gas operated, semi-automatic rifle. It was found with many others in the A Shau Valley, still wrapped in grease, and I don't think it has ever been fired. I removed the bolt and placed it in the bottom of my seabag before leaving California, and as far as I know, the closest place to find ammunition for it is in Communist China. I have all the proper documentation to bring it home and have never tried to conceal it in any way."

"Wrap it up in this," he said, handing me some newspaper and clear tape.

"You won't have any further problems from rookie cops today." His voice softened just a little, and he took a step back as he said, "I served with the Corps. I recognize the insignia on your arm. Welcome home. I'm glad you made it back in one piece, Doc. Good luck to you." And he saluted.

I returned his salute and complied with his advice. It still looked a lot like a rifle, only now it was wrapped in a newspaper. He called one of his cars to give me a ride back up to the North Terminal. When they dropped me off, it was about 6:00 a.m., so I decided to go to the South Terminal. It was close to a mile of walking, but my little inner voice said that was where Harriet would be looking for me. I was traveling heavy, and it took me about a half hour to get there. Since it was still early, not too many people were around; I took a chair where I could relax and have a good view of the terminal floor. The personnel at the counters were arriving and setting up. A few people were coming in from the parking lot to catch their early morning flight.

My eyes kept sweeping the ever-more crowded floor when I saw her. She was moving across the terminal toward the counters on those gorgeous legs and reading the incoming flight board. She had on a beautiful pink dress that she had hand-sewn from a fabric called marshmallow cream. She had pink sweetheart roses pinned to her handbag. She was then, and is now, the best-looking woman I have ever known. I got up and began to move in her direction. Her attention was focused on the incoming flight boards and finding the shortest line to ask when the flights from California were coming in. As I moved to intersect her path, I finally came into her field of vision, and she spotted me.

"Hi, beautiful," I said.

After ten months, it was absolutely wonderful to hold her in my arms again. We picked up all my belongings and walked hand in hand into the sunshine of that beautiful, clear, late April morning.

# EPILOGUE

Like many returning servicemen during that time in this country, I remained very quiet and set about resuming my life. In my first month home, I reconnected with family and a few old friends. I bought a 1969 Chevy Nova, Phantom Green, with a black interior. I found a job with a small steel company, and, thanks to the GI Bill, re-enrolled in college.

By chance or fate, the college I was attending was in the process of opening a School of Nursing. So I got to thinking again that I knew quite a lot about health care and was even pretty good at it. One late summer day, I walked across the campus to the new school's office and spoke with the dean of the program. There I started a career that has spanned over forty years and has produced enough stories for another whole book. At times, it still involves working specifically with my fellow veterans who are suffering from posttraumatic stress disorder and/or substance abuse issues.

I know I have to answer the question: Did he get the girl? Yes, he did. Harriet and I had a beautiful December wedding that year. Three years later, we had our first son Peter John, and two years after that, Andrew Christian was born. We have had the opportunity to live and work in several very beautiful places over the years. We have had many wonderful experiences and made countless friends from the mountains of California and Colorado to the shores of Lake Michigan.

The boys are grown now, and Harriet and I are proud grandparents to Christian Alexander Holm, another of the great experiences in our lives. We currently live a delightfully quiet life together with our English Setter, Beamer, in the Blue Ridge Mountains of Southwestern Virginia. Living the dream, we own a small white home with a picket fence and roses in front and a backyard full of flower gardens. I am still an active Registered Nurse, still trying to stamp out disease and illness, forty plus hours a week. My spare time is spent keeping up with the house and gardens, hunting for grouse (in season) with Beamer, model railroading, and, oh yes, writing these stories.

My parents did receive the empty envelope with the hurried message. At first, my mother said she thought it was a bad joke, but they eventually found the written message inside.

I am still the only veteran I know who was never issued a set of dog tags.

Over the years, I have found a few of my buddies from Vietnam. We keep in touch occasionally through phone calls, the Internet, and snail mail. We have become husbands, fathers, and grandfathers. We all carry around a few more pounds, more gray hairs, and a lot more wisdom. To this day, the bonds of brotherhood and friendship we formed in that faraway place and time are still strong and cherished. It makes me feel good to know that what I was able to do while with them made a difference.

CPSIA information can be obtained at www.ICGtesting.com
Printed in the USA
BVOW041713120313

315362BV00001B/3/P